ADVANCE PRAISE FOR

TRANSFORMATIVE POTENTIAL-BASED RESEARCH

A Guide to Successfully Finding One's Place in Research

"In *Transformative Potential-Based Research: A Guide to Successfully Finding One's Place in Research*, Harvey and Moroz provide educators whose research identities are just being formed a way to frame their work in notions of potential instead of traditional 'problems of practice'. They guide the reader in situating their potential research in their passions and own positionality while also providing a challenge to examine our own epistemologies and reflexivity in purposeful communities of support. Incredibly useful are the reflective exercises that conclude each chapter. They begin by moving the reader from a desire to find the 'perfect topic' to ideas that 'puzzle us' and end with reflective prompts that help the reader to ultimately tell the story of their research findings."

Katie Pekel, Ed.D.,
Executive Director of Educational Leadership,
University of Minnesota

"*Transformational Potential-Based Research: A Guide to Successfully Finding One's Place in Research* is like a strong rope guiding new researchers up a challenging climb. It offers the stability and support needed to navigate the unfamiliar landscape of academic research. Each chapter is a checkpoint, establishing the researcher's mindset in understanding positionality and encouraging a potential-based journey. Harvey and Moroz provide supportive activities, helping researchers find their balance while connecting with a supportive community. With thoughtful guidance, it leads the researcher to the peak, where they can confidently reach their potential."

Kim Hiel, Ed.D.,
Superintendent, Osseo Area Schools;
Adjunct Professor, Hamline University

"An engaging and innovative approach to design and the transformative power of research, this is compelling reading for practitioners and the general public alike. The text incorporates key features of adult learning theory, using narrative to draw the reader in, situating chapters within their proper context, and demonstrating the power of scholarly narrative to engage learners in developing and strengthening their own professional voices.

Each chapter includes activities that provide the reader with a vehicle for engaging with the ideas, constructing knowledge, and making explicit connections to their own research. The chapters end with reflective activities to deepen understanding of the text. I highly recommend it."

Vivian Johnson, PhD,
Professor emeritus,
Hamline School of Education and Leadership

"*Transformative Potential-Based Research: A Guide to Successfully Finding One's Place in Research* provides a structured framework that encourages researchers to shift their mindset from deficit-based thinking to one focused on opportunities. The Potential-Based Research Framework allows researchers to explore new possibilities and innovative ideas by incorporating critical thinking, positionality, and community expertise. In a time when public conversations around education tend to emphasize problems, this book brings a refreshing and hopeful perspective to educational research."

Sara B. Ewell,
Northeastern University

"Harvey and Moroz truly understand what it means to "find one's place" in the research world. By sharing their scholarly journey, the book takes the reader on a research adventure, offering a road map that empowers and instructs scholars as they learn to find their own place. In the demanding and ever-changing world of research, this book serves as an essential companion, friend, and practical guide that carries and inspires scholars."

Dr. Jill Long,
Associate Professor and Education Program Director,
The College of St. Scholastica,
and EdD Hamline University Graduate

"*Transformative Potential-Based Research* has the potential to become the core support for EdD students. I was absorbed with every page, and Trish and Karen did a brilliant job weaving their extended professional experiences with broader examples and research. I also like the meaningful activities they include in each chapter."

Kristie O'Brien,
Director of Learning and Teaching,
Winona Public Schools (MN) & EdD graduate student,
Hamline University

TRANSFORMATIVE POTENTIAL-BASED RESEARCH

The Coming of Age of the Education Doctorate

Edited by Jill Alexa Perry, PhD

The mission of The Coming of Age of the Education Doctorate series is to present volumes of research and work focused on the improvement of the Education Doctorate (EdD) and, over the course of the past 14 years, that faculty and schools of education around the U.S. and the world have made to professionalize this degree for the advanced preparation of educational practitioners. Specifically, this series will highlight efforts to improve the purpose, curriculum, and milestone experiences of the degree, in addition to highlighting the work of those who have graduated from redesigned EdD programs. The series will consist of print books, e-books, and fractional digital content for faculty, pre-service teachers, practitioners, and libraries.

Upcoming titles in the series

Challenges in (Re)designing EdD Programs: Supporting Change with Learning Cases
edited by Jill A. Perry (2023)
Reclaiming the Education Doctorate: A Guidebook for Preparing Scholarly Practitioners
by Jill A. Perry (2023)
Teaching Critical Inquiry and Applied Research in EdD Programs: Moving Beyond Traditional Methods
by Christopher Benedetti and Amanda Covarrubias (2023)
Transforming Identities: How EdD Programs Develop Practitioners into Scholar-Practitioners
edited by Stephen J. Pape, Camille L. Bryant, Ranjini Mahinda JohnBull, and Karen S. Karp (2023)
Innovation and Impact: The Origins and Elements of EdD Program Excellence
edited by W. Kyle Ingle and Harriette Thurber Rasmussen (2024)
The IMPACT of the Scholarly Practitioner Doctorate: Exercising Socially Just Leadership and Making Equitable Change
edited by Stephanie Smith Budhai and Deanna Hill (2024)
The Importance of the Dissertation in Practice (DiP): A Resource Guide for EdD Students, Their Committee Members and Advisors, and Departmental and University Leaders Involved with EdD Programs
by Kimberlee Everson, Kelly M. Torres, Lynn Hemmer, and Suha Tamim (2024)
The Disquisition: An Equity-Driven Capstone for Leadership Preparation Programs
by Jess Weiler and Emily Virtue (2024)
Transformative Potential-Based Research: A Guide to Successfully Finding One's Place in Research
by Trish Harvey and Karen Moroz (2025)
Social Justice Praxis in EdD Programs
by Ignacio Hernández and Alexia Theresa Pimentel (2025)

Writing as Becoming: EdD Students Learning to Write as Scholarly Practitioners
by Veselina S. Lambrev and Micki M. Caskey (2025)
Walk the Social Justice Talk:
Designing, Implementing, and Advancing an Empowering EdD Doctorate
by Cathy Ikeda, Walter Kaumoku III, and Lori Ideta (2026)
The Power of I: Using First-Person Writing to Define and Develop the EdD Writer
by Harriette T. Rasmussen, Deanna Hill, Peggy Kong, Ellana Black,
and Bruce Levine (2026)

Dr. Jill Alexa Perry is the Executive Director of the Carnegie Project on the Educational Doctorate (CPED) and an Associate Professor of Practice in the Educational Foundations, Organizations and Policy at the University of Pittsburgh. If you have a proposal that you wish to have considered for publication in the series, please send a full prospectus and CV to Dr. Perry at jillaperry@cped.org.

DEDICATION

A huge thank-you to our trusted colleague, Dr. Vivian Johnson, who provided thoughtful feedback throughout the writing process. Her commitment to education continues to shine through all she does.

Thank you, as always, to our families, Teri, Tate, and Teigen (Trish), and Ella and Ava (Karen). You continue to climb the mountains with us—supporting our work and making our journey so enjoyable.

TRANSFORMATIVE POTENTIAL-BASED RESEARCH

A Guide to Successfully Finding
One's Place in Research

BY
TRISH HARVEY AND KAREN MOROZ

Myers Education Press
GORHAM, MAINE

Published by Myers Education Press, LLC
P.O. Box 424 Gorham, ME 04038

Myers Education Press is an academic publisher specializing in books, e-books, and digital content in the field of education. All of our books are subjected to a rigorous peer review process and produced in compliance with the standards of the Council on Library and Information Resources.

Library of Congress Cataloging-in-Publication Data available from Library of Congress.

13-digit ISBN 978-1-9755-0701-5 (paperback)
13-digit ISBN 978-1-9755-0702-2 (library networkable e-edition)
13-digit ISBN 978-1-9755-0703-9 (consumer e-edition)

Printed in the United States of America.

All first editions printed on acid-free paper that meets the American National Standards Institute Z39-48 standard.

Cover design by Teresa Lagrange.

CONTENTS

LIST OF FIGURES AND TABLES

List of Figures

List of Tables

INTRODUCTION

THIS TEXT HAS BEEN an inspiring and intense journey in thinking about how our students, primarily practitioners in the field of education, select their research topics, and how we can best support them in this work. Initially, we started writing this text for a book series on problem-based learning approaches. Neither of us come to our work with a deficit mindset about schooling or public education, and the focus of identifying problems in crafting a research topic was not resonating with our beliefs, experiences, and practices. After much reflection and conversation, we realized that a "potential-based approach" not only aligned better with our own beliefs, but it is also much needed in a post-pandemic educational world. We realized that a potential-based approach was missing from the existing literature. We asked ourselves, what if we stop looking for problems? What if we start looking for the potential in our settings, in all our students, and in our own work?

It is not a simple "switch" but one we believe must be explored in earnest with tangible approaches deployed that help to shift thinking. Educators, for many understandable reasons, have been programmed to fix problems. As such, many go through their days looking for problems, labeling who or what is to blame, and knowingly or unknowingly promoting deficit thinking. This problem-based approach can lead to unconsciously promoting inequities by placing the "blame" on certain groups of people or focusing solely on gaps and underperformance. In doing so, we limit our own creativity and contribute to the narrative that education is only comprised of complex problems. A focus on problems creates extreme pressure on ourselves and others to be fixers. Additionally, as Brookfield (1995) argued, focusing on problems in research without a reflective process causes researchers to "tend to accept the blame for problems that are not of [their] own making" (p. 2). The very definition of "problem" includes the words "harmful" and "unwelcome." Why would we want to begin the very important work of educational research with pessimism and cynicism?

It is time to recognize that there have been and can be serious consequences when we only see problems. We believe that by framing our work and our research as potential-based, we can allow the consumers of our research to see value in our topics and to seek their own potential-based mindsets. Framing your research study towards the potential of a situation or circumstance requires you to address the system, to consider the process and steps forward, and to fully engage your stakeholders in the study. We have created a theory that guides researchers through this shift. It is a theory that can be applied to qualitative, quantitative, and mixed methods research projects.

Our theory asks you to climb the research mountain with us. To help you do so, we will share our own experiences in doing research and in working with students (from pre-kindergarten to doctoral level). Our combined years of experience, our passion for all things education, and our commitment to student growth/transformation served as the pillars in the development of this book and theory. We look forward to helping readers identify and explore potential-based topics that tap into important ways of thinking and acting, and we encourage all to settle into the process—taking time to make sure the eventual research study truly reflects what you want to do and where the potential exists. Indeed, it is an example of needing to go slow to go fast, a skill that many of us have not afforded ourselves time to perfect. Our typical day-to-day work demands quick thinking, ongoing decision making, and the ability to meet the varied needs of those around us. We invite you to fight those tendencies. Through this text and its reflective activities, we ask you to slow down and consider all aspects of a topic. You, your topic, and the field of education will benefit from this approach.

So . . . let's climb the mountain . . .

Reference

Brookfield, S. D. (1995). *Becoming a critically reflective teacher.* Jossey-Bass.

CHAPTER ONE

Introduction: The Journey

THE CLICHÉD STATEMENT OF life not being about the destination but rather about the journey moves beyond being "just" a cliché when one really stops to analyze and treasure their own journey. In doing so one notices big and not-so-big moments in their professional life that impact who they are as a person, a researcher, and a scholar. It is important, then, that we all take time to deeply reflect on our own journeys as educators and researchers and that we find ways to encourage others to do the same. Only when this happens can we properly position ourselves in the world of research . . . a world where potential for great change exists and where we are allowed to add our voices and our own journeys to the professional discourse. As we begin this book, then, we share our own journeys so that our positionality, passions, and places in teaching and research are clear to readers who will, in subsequent chapters, be guided through their own journeys with the goal of fully understanding and embracing their roles as educators and researchers who embody a potential-based learning approach, a concept that will be further explored.

We share our own journeys because they impact how we approach the work, and communicating them is "central to how we create meaning in our own lives, and . . . how we put meanings into motion in our academic research as well" (Bochner & Ellis, 2016, p. 36). Your journey will impact how you approach the research, and we believe this text will guide you as you move forward. The purpose we have in writing this text is to help educators and researchers be successful. We believe the journey in finding your research question can be a transformative and reflective process. In finding your research question, you can also reaffirm your own purpose and the "why" in your work; you can truly find your place in research.

Karen's Journey

In my role as associate professor in the School of Education and Leadership at Hamline University in St. Paul, MN, it is a joy to work with practitioners who are motivated to continue improving their ability to impact students, colleagues, and the educational system as a whole. As an instructor in a fairly small master's and doctoral program, I am afforded the opportunity to work with many adult students more than once as they progress through their programs. Doing so allows me to watch as their view of their professional selves shifts, with many transitioning from "I want to know what others have to say about this" to "I have something to say about this!" As students engage in critical reflection and structured inquiry, their approach to research topics also shifts from "It is interesting to me that . . ." to full-blown capstones and dissertations where they are fully immersed in the research and excited to add their voice to the educational research base. In introductory courses, conversations center around topic identification, narrowing of scope, and confidence building as educators learn to look at themselves as action researchers primed to explore relevant issues and to add to the professional discourse. In subsequent advanced courses, those action researchers contribute to the professional discourse in important ways, and I am fortunate enough to be part of their journeys, learning so much myself along the way about critical current issues impacting individuals and communities.

Prior to teaching full-time in higher education, I was fortunate enough to spend 15 years as a seventh-grade language arts teacher where much of my work focused on nurturing the writing skills of young adolescents, while interestingly little time focused on nurturing myself as a writer. It was within those classroom walls, though, where much of my interest about what it means to be an action researcher was developed, as I not only supported my students through what it meant to be a writer but also became more and more intrigued by what it meant to really understand the young people I was working with and how that deepened understanding could allow me to have an even greater impact on them.

It was with that interest that one of my most memorable experiences as a middle-level educator was born. In my fifth year of teaching, I was feeling good about what I was doing; I was enjoying the students; I was in a master's program and continuing to learn more about what it means to really teach. I recall, to this day, the day my first publication began. My students and I were engaged in a great discussion about a text, and their responses were leaving me more and more intrigued about who they really were and where they saw themselves fitting into our larger world. I "pushed aside" the curriculum for a bit and we "just" talked . . . about them, about being teenagers, about our world. They had voices and wanted to be heard. The next day I followed up with that group, the conversations not over and in my mind deserving to be captured. The students were excited about my proposal, and for the next month, we turned our room into a publishing center with students dividing tasks and undertaking the exciting and cathartic experience of writing about their views on social issues. The end result was a self-published anthology, *Life Through the Eyes of Teens*. Twenty-five years later this is still one of the most transformative experiences of my professional journey. Without labeling it as such at that time, it was my first true experience as an action researcher, and the impact it had on my career was profound.

My idea of doing research, up until that time, had been based on my life as an English major and a teacher who helped students research topics of interest. I did not realize at the time that I could be, and was, a researcher—an action researcher, day in and day out—and that "doing research" could go, and should go, well beyond reading and synthesizing what others had written about a topic. Instead, I needed to live within my environment as a researcher. I needed to take questions of interest, much like I had with *Life Through the Eyes of Teens*, and explore them in a way that allowed me to collect data, develop my own ideas, and become part of the professional discourse.

This understanding was further supported and nurtured during my doctoral program where we were encouraged to see every aspect of life and profession through a researcher's lens. Through the program I questioned my role as an educator and worked to explore those questions with my students, my colleagues, my doctoral classmates and instructors, and other communities. I became an action researcher, and I think once you have that perception of yourself, it is part of all you do.

Knowing how my shift in self-perception has impacted my career has led to one of my key professional goals—that of helping graduate students see themselves as action researchers. I want my students to know that they are not only developing their own skills as educators and researchers but also contributing to others' growth as they share publicly, in small or big ways, much like my seventh graders did during that exciting publishing adventure.

Trish's Journey

Although I am not sure what I want to be when I "grow up," my current role is as an associate professor in the School of Education at Hamline University in St. Paul, MN. I work with graduate students pursuing their master's degree in education or their educational doctorate degree. I have worked with hundreds of students who were completing their culminating papers, including capstone theses, master's research papers, capstone projects, and dissertations.

When I think about the most rewarding parts of my work, it is working with these students on their research projects. Helping students find their passion, working to create a research agenda, designing a study, and publishing the results is a transformative process. Whether my students are studying their classrooms, their communities, their organizations, and/or a new approach, strategy, or tool, I have witnessed and believe that a structured inquiry process helps students to reconnect with their original "why" for being in the field of education, while also creating a path to the future.

Prior to working at Hamline, I held a number of different positions. My earliest roles were in economic development until I found my passion for working in the classroom. My first teaching position was in a small town, with a young staff and an inspiring principal. Because we were a small district, everyone wore many hats, and my teaching job expanded into coaching, assessment work, and district leadership. I taught every social studies subject to ninth-through-twelfth graders, but my main assignment was ninth-grade American history. I assigned and read hundreds of five-paragraph essays on the Civil War—and I learned how to make history relevant to my students. Most importantly, I was surrounded by smart, hard-working, and passionate colleagues. We collaborated on interdisciplinary units, we implemented new approaches with eagerness, and we had the freedom to experiment in our classrooms. Standardized testing was just beginning.

After this first teaching position, I spent a few years in higher education in Wisconsin, working with teachers earning their master's degrees in education. Our program traveled to a school and offered a two-year weekend program. For the culminating project, program participants implemented an action research project and collected data. The program was extremely successful—and when I reflect on why it was successful, it might be a combination of affordability and accessibility, but I truly think we helped teachers rediscover their passion and "why" for teaching. Through a community and constructivist approach, we asked educators to research a topic and experiment in their classrooms with a focus on improving student learning. These studies were inspiring and transformational for these educators. I watched my students evolve into teacher leaders through the structured inquiry process. I loved this work but yearned to be back in K-12 schools, so returned to middle school.

My second K-12 teaching position was working in a middle school with eighth graders. In the short time that I had been out of the K-12 classroom, two things had significantly changed. First, standardized testing had changed the prioritization of subjects. As a social studies teacher, my content area was not tested and instead, I was tasked with making reading and reading comprehension a focus of my work. Second, technology had exploded, and there were so many new ways to access content and engage students. Again, I worked with an amazing team of middle school educators—student-focused, hard-working, and committed.

One example I like to share is that every year, we dedicated the spring to working collaboratively on an interdisciplinary approach to History Day projects with students. I have always argued that History Day was one of the best project-based activities I was involved in as a middle school teacher. Students had a chance to choose their topic, select the type of project they wanted to create, and choose their work-group. Students spent six months researching, synthesizing, and creating for their final projects. The resulting research projects, on display at our History Day Celebration, were always phenomenal examples of student inquiry.

One additional work experience I had was serving as a digital learning coordinator for a large school district. I was tasked with implementing 1:1 iPads in several classrooms, along with adopting a new learning management system, moving several high school classes online, and helping teachers to rethink how to use technology in their classrooms. When teachers saw me, I typically had one of two responses—teachers were either excited to see me or quickly closed their door. Change is hard!

And now, I am starting my tenth year at Hamline University. I love my work with graduate students in education. I bring my own past experiences and beliefs into my work. I believe it is important for teachers to have some freedom in the classroom; I know it is important to have strong colleagues, and I maintain that teachers need a student-centered "why" to be successful.

Framework

We share our own journeys because they impact how we approach this work. We resonate with the following passage from Bochner and Ellis (2016), who acknowledged the intersection of the researcher and the researched:

> Many of us were drawn to a life of research by our lived experience of emotional epiphanies that changed or deeply affected us. We believe that these experiences are worthy of observation, examination, and reflection. We also believe that these experiences strongly influence our perceptions and interpretation of other people's lives. (p. 50)

Your journey will impact how you approach the research, and we believe this text will guide you as you move forward. Finding your place in research is important, but it can also be scary. We are well aware that the role of researcher can indeed be daunting at times because even when properly supported, researchers who have identified topics of real meaning can feel immense pressure to "get it right." It is not uncommon at all for individuals to experience feeling like impostors in the world of educational research. More about this feeling of being an impostor will be shared in Chapter Four, focusing on mindsets.

It is our hope that this book will support instructors and students through all stages of research including:

- identifying and embracing relevant and essential topics,
- crafting research questions that accurately and concisely convey the purpose(s),
- exploring one's own connection to the issue,
- developing and employing individual processes that lead to success, and
- determining a potential-based frame that motivates the writer and frames the work.

To reach these goals, it is important that readers understand the intent and structure of this text and of each individual chapter; doing so will help one determine how to best use this text.

The primary goal of this text is to provide students with a process for learning how to develop a potential-based inquiry approach to their research and to reenvision themselves as researchers, scholars, and leaders who can contribute to the professional conversation. To guide this work we have developed a framework (see Figure 1.1). We invite readers to review the mountain metaphor shared within the framework and to keep the visual present at all times as they progress through the book. It will be addressed often, and readers will be invited to use, extend, and discuss it numerous times throughout their journeys.

Figure 1.1 *Potential-Based Research Framework*

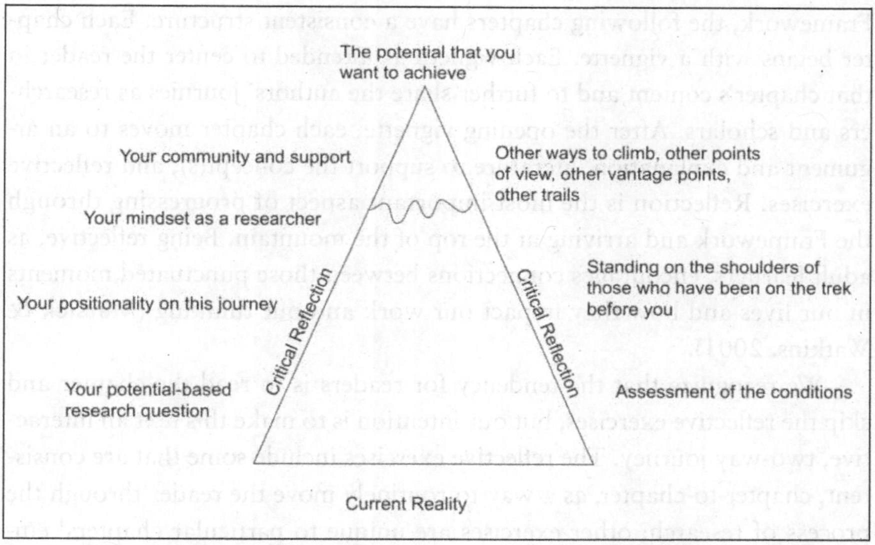

The Potential-Based Research Framework challenges you to approach research with a paradigm shift away from problem-solving toward seeing where potential exists and finding ways to reach it. The current reality sits at the bottom, and the potential exists at the top. Along the journey, the researcher asks questions that confront the current reality but also contain an element of curiosity around "what could be." The journey requires an assessment of the current conditions and an exhaustive review of existing literature on the topic. Climbing does require expertise! You will even challenge yourself to consider other viewpoints and to welcome perspectives that you might disagree with. The quest also asks you to examine and identify your own positionality on the topic, your mindset, and your community of support.

On this journey, take time to *wallow*. This is a term a colleague shared years ago when talking about the research process—and although the term might make you think about pigs wallowing in the mud, the premise works. Take time to sit back, reflect, talk to colleagues, breathe, let your topic breathe, and sit in the muddy messiness of your topic. And similar to real hiking, everyone has their own pace. It is your own journey to the top.

Conclusion

In addition to developing and explaining the Potential-Based Research Framework, the following chapters have a consistent structure. Each chapter begins with a vignette. Each vignette is intended to center the reader in that chapter's content and to further share the authors' journies as researchers and scholars. After the opening vignette, each chapter moves to an argument and explanation, literature to support the concept(s), and reflective exercises. Reflection is the most important aspect of progressing through the Framework and arriving at the top of the mountain. Being reflective, as adult learners, encourages connections between those punctuated moments in our lives and how they impact our work and our thinking (Marsick & Watkins, 2001).

We recognize that the tendency for readers is to read the chapter and skip the reflective exercises, but our intention is to make this text an interactive, two-way journey. The reflective exercises include some that are consistent, chapter-to-chapter, as a way to routinely move the reader through the process of research; other exercises are unique to particular chapters' emphases. How the reflective exercises are used can vary. It may be helpful to complete some individually, while others will be most effective if completed or discussed collaboratively. All are derived from our work with students, and many are based on activities or approaches that we experienced as researchers or students ourselves.

By centering yourself in the chapter's focus, exploring key literature related to that focus, and then committing to each of the reflective exercises, you as reader will feel comfortable engaging in transformative potential-based research. The research will feel less daunting, and the structured inquiry process itself will indeed feel accessible. In the end, it is the goal that you will know that your journey has prepared you to tackle your current passions through research.

Let's begin the climb.

Note. Rigby, 2022

References

Bochner, A. & Ellis, C. (2016). *Evocative autoethnography: Writing lives and telling stories.* Routledge.

Marsick, V. J., & Watkins, K. E. (2001). Informal and incidental learning. In S. B. Merriam (Ed.), *The new update on adult learning theory* (Vol. 89) (pp. 25–34). Jossey-Bass.

Rigby, W. (2022, July 20). *Photo gallery: Hike of the week – Western Ute Trail provides amazing views* [Photograph]. *Estes Park Trail Gazette.* https://www.eptrail.com/2022/07/20/photo-gallery-hike-of-the-week-western-ute-trail-provides-amazing-views/

CHAPTER TWO

What Do You Care About? Why? Where is the Potential?

Picture books have long been a part of my (Karen's) teaching approach; it only makes sense, then, that as I work to discover topics to research and as I work to help students do the same, I would turn to a picture book, ***Kiyoshi's Walk*** *(Karlins, 2021). The text, one described as turning art into observation, introduces readers to a young boy who asks his grandfather, a prolific writer, where all his poems come from. His grandfather doesn't respond with an exact answer but rather closes his current writing project and takes his curious grandson on a walk. As they wander through their community, Eto pointing out the "simple" everyday occurrences all around them that can be put to paper, Kiyoshi comes to realize that ideas for writing "'come from here,'. . . and open[s] his arms wide to take in the river and the sky and the distant buildings. 'And they come from here,' he said, and pointed to his own heart." (p. 25)*

Note. Karlins, 2021

What Do You Care About and Where is the Potential?: Argument and Explanation

While the child in this picture book is not digging into deep issues that need to be explored, the same concept of "ideas are all around us" does hold true for us as teachers, educational leaders, and researchers as we work to identify topics we care about and whether those topics warrant exploration. Block (2003) echoed this sentiment as he explained that in research, "the paradoxical questions that lead us to what matters most are those familiar, persistent, complicated questions about our lives, individually and organizationally, that defy clear solutions" (p. 16). We also advocate that in addition to attributes of paradoxical questions described by Block (2003), our students pay attention to the potential of their questions. The reality is, you are going to live with this research for a significant amount of time. It is going to wake you up at night, and you are going to find yourself pulling over to the side of the road to "make note of this idea before I forget." Can one take any topic, push through, and complete a project without having a strong passion for it? Sure. Is it much more enjoyable and rewarding to spend the necessary hours and intellectual capacity focused on a topic in which one is interested in becoming completely immersed, truly discovering new ideas and potential that can contribute to the professional discourse? Absolutely! With that in mind, this chapter asks readers to explore what it is they really care about and to "trust that doing work that [gives] meaning to [their] life and has the potential to offer meaning to and evoke meaning in others is important" (Bochner & Ellis, 2016, p. 30). As you explore ideas around which to center research and writing, keep in mind the importance of choosing something that is within your locus of control, one with a scope that is manageable.

Knowing the amount of energy you will spend within this potential-based learning experience, it can feel overwhelming to try to come up with the "perfect" area of inquiry to explore. and it is true that identifying your research topic is a critical—perhaps the most critical—part of the process.

We encourage you, however, to not set out initially with an intent to find the perfect topic, but rather to take time to live within your professional environment with a heightened awareness of aspects within that environment that need attention or that are puzzling to you. Allow yourself to do a *Kiyoshi's Walk* (Karlins, 2021). As you examine your own professional setting with a heightened awareness of who you are as a researcher, you will begin seeing potential everywhere because, as Bochner and Ellis (2016) stated, when we "choose to study life in its natural settings, to think aesthetically . . . and concentrate on meanings [we can be taken] into the heart of the lived experience" (p. 34).

Historically, viewing topics as potential has not been the first thing people do, but we are adamant that for our profession to thrive and create strong change, we must flip the narrative from being problem-based to embracing potential in what had been seen as "issues." While this concept of shifting from problem-based to potential-based will be further explored in Chapter Four, for now we feel it is important to state that potential-based topics may be obvious, or they may be more nuanced. They may be based on ideas that have been discussed for years among colleagues, or they may arise in that moment that you are in front of a class or in a meeting and you think, "Why am I feeling this way? What is making me look at this differently than I have before or seemingly different from how others are looking at the topic?" Topics worth exploring are those that take your career, your educational setting, or the individuals most directly impacted by the type of answers or change you are pursuing to the next level. When you select the right topic, it might even feel like "cheating" because the research is entrenched in your day-to-day work to improve your current conditions. Through the research, communication about, and deepened understanding of these areas of your professional life, you are able to create "conversations with [yourself] and your readers" (Bochner & Ellis, 2016, p. 36) that push boundaries and influence the thoughts and actions of you as the researcher, of your participants, and of those that read your work.

For example, as I (Karen) was exploring my own professional world while in my doctoral program, hoping to find a worthy topic for my dissertation, I rotated through ideas, but none really seemed to "stick." They all felt like ideas that I "should" be studying, yet none motivated me, and my frustration mounted. Fortunately, I knew enough to stop trying so hard. I knew I was writing within a program that truly believed in the constructive approach to teaching and learning and that there wasn't one "right" topic. One day—I actually remember it quite vividly, even all these years later—I was standing in front of my seventh graders with a seven-month-old at home and realized I was looking at those seventh graders differently than I had for the past nine years. I was treating them differently. I was teaching differently. I was different . . . and now, I was curious. With this curiosity,

I started reflecting on my day-to-day and realizing that somehow the transition to new parenthood was impacting my teaching philosophy and classroom practices. I didn't understand it and I didn't immediately realize I had landed on a research topic. The idea stuck with me though, and I eventually talked it through with my advisors. Fortunately, they encouraged me to explore the idea. What resulted was a case study of veteran female teachers who became first-time parents. As a researcher, I looked specifically at shifts in teaching philosophies and classroom practices, and through a survey, interview, and focus group, I found that indeed there were commonalities in experiences. I remained committed to the research, in large part because it was helping me better understand the "new" me. In hindsight, I believe that it was also allowing me to find and then share the potential that lies in life transitions if we are willing to frame them as transitions that impact our lives in positive ways (potential-based) rather than as experiences that add additional stress (problem-based). My dissertation research was different, but it mattered to me and it mattered to others who, through being a part of my study and/or reading the end result, were able to see themselves in that research and to become conscious of the ways transitions impact an educator's philosophies and practices.

Literature: Identifying a Research Focus

Work, such as my journey as just described, followed Boyer's (1996) advice as he encouraged researchers to question phenomena and to acquire and disseminate knowledge, providing five centering approaches to the identification of topic. Table 2.1 shares how we see the connections between Boyer's aspects of scholarship and our potential-based framework. The best of all potential-based topics will dip its toes into many or all of Boyer's aspects of scholarship, but we share a specific example for each aspect in order to illustrate how the shift to potential-based thinking plays out in actual research topics.

As you seek that type of topic, do not rush through the process. Talk to others; keep lists and lists and more lists; allow your professional brain to dream and take on those tasks that you have perhaps thought of as "too big of an issue for just one person to change." But then *be* that one person.

Table 2.1 *Connections: Boyer et al.'s Scholarship and Potential-Based Research*

Boyer et al.'s (2015) Scholarship	Potential-Based Research Examples
The scholarship of discovery: Knowledge acquired through research—"disciplined investigative efforts" (p. 81) in the pursuit of new intellectual knowledge.	Case study dissertation work on early childhood education in Ethiopian schools in order to understand the potential for improving these schools and learning opportunities for three-five years olds.
The scholarship of integration: Knowledge acquired through synthesis—"making connections across the disciplines" (p. 82); serious disciplined work that seeks to interpret, draw together, and bring new insight to bear on original research.	Research focused on gathering the perceptions of parents of elementary school English Language Learners (ELLs) regarding the potential for collaboration between public elementary schools and county public libraries for improving the literacy of ELLs in rural communities.
The scholarship of application: Knowledge acquired through practice—"new intellectual understandings can arise out of the very act of application" (p. 85).	Action research study where a doctoral student sees the potential in rewriting an American Literature curriculum using Black Literature to engage her students and promote social justice.
The scholarship of teaching: Knowledge acquired through teaching—a dynamic endeavor between teachers and learners that increases capacities for reflection, critical, and creative thinking and action.	Qualitative research study researching the environmental justice movement to determine how social justice intersects with pressing global issues commonly found in environmental science curriculum. Identified the potential for environmental science educators to integrate social justice themes in their classrooms and how environmental education evolved to incorporate climate change education.
The scholarship of engagement: Knowledge acquired within any of the above four scholarships through activities that connect the academic with people and places outside the campus and which ultimately direct the work of the academy toward larger, "more humane ends" (p. 127).	Phenomenological study of the School Resource Officer (SRO) and Principal Partnership. The increased presence of School Resource Officers (SROs) in schools places them in direct contact with school principals. This study explored the potential benefits of partnership between SROs and principals in six public secondary schools.

This is your chance to take on the topic from those lists and your professional dreaming. Choose the topic that does not leave you alone! Start with a broad idea, and then work to narrow your focus. Consider using the following criteria to analyze the critical and contemporary discourse around your potential topic. (Note: You will be guided through these criteria within the reflective activities.)

- Consider your own core beliefs about the goals, methods, and purpose of education.
- Explore the social, cognitive, economic, and political elements of teaching and learning.
- Investigate the dominant narratives that influence education in your field.
- Identify areas of *potential* in your field.
- Consider potential pedagogical connections.
- Think about the multiple perspectives surrounding the issue.
- Determine and contemplate what you see as the greatest challenge and/or ramification of the issue.
- Explore the historical context of this issue.

With much of the work of brainstorming done, it is critical, at this point, that you take time to look at how you frame your work, consciously addressing the issue in a manner that looks at systems that create areas that need attention and allow you to truly take a potential-based approach rather than work to "fix a problem." This is essential, for as Davis and Museus (2019) stated,

> Education is a problem-based field, [and therefore] students are encouraged to use problems to justify the urgency of their research. To be sure, there are numerous problems plaguing education, but how problems are identified and named is just as important to the research process as efforts to actually address them. Research itself becomes problematic when framed with deficit thinking, and researchers are not immune to using deficit frames to respond to educational issues. (p. 1)

Our goal is to shift the deficit frames to potential-based frames. We argue that education does not need to be a problem-based field, but rather a potential-based field, where researchers can celebrate their connections to the topic and interest in the topic. Using our framework, researchers can stop perpetuating deficit mindsets and replace them with their own critical contemplation of the issues and propose recommendations for their resolution based on research. By keeping these points in mind you are able to do research that,

> address[es] pressing issues. Research should also involve an interest that can be sustained. All choices need to be grounded in the literature from related fields. The more definite descriptors are, the more targeted the literature review and the more focused the research and subsequent writing. (Dowell et al., 2022, p. 7)

Potential-based research provides the space for addressing pressing issues without a deficit mindset or placing blame. As Jane B. (2022) noted, "We need to stop seeing what is missing but look at what students do have" ("Correcting the Deficit in Critical Thinking" section). The goal is to identify where the potential exists and to develop a targeted study focused on how to achieve it.

From a Research Topic to a Research Question

With a list of potential-based topics identified, it is now time to craft questions that will guide your work. You owe it to yourself to create space to formulate strong research questions, knowing that they may shift as your research unfolds, and to remind yourself that "questions open the door to the future and are more powerful than answers" (Block, 2018, p. 192).

Block (2018), in talking about creating a strong community, offered some interesting suggestions about questions that each individual brings to a group. While offered in a different sense than as a researcher, his suggestions are still helpful to address in the early stages of your question development. Block reminded us that great questions,

> [require] each person to bring their own, personal meaning to the room and that . . . [a]ll passion, commitment, and connection grow out of what is

> most personal. We need to create space for the personal. It evokes anxiety. All that matters makes us anxious. It is our wish to escape from anxiety that steals our aliveness. If there is no edge to the question, there is no power. (p. 110)

How, though, do you create that type of edgy question? Our suggestion is to craft a long list of questions and to allow yourself time to brainstorm. Then, let that brainstorming sit a bit before revisiting the list and looking at those questions as if you are going to pursue them as a line of inquiry. As you analyze each with that lens, apply the following criteria to strengthen your research question(s). Later in this chapter's reflective activities, you will be guided to analyze each question using the suggested criteria more thoroughly. This is great practice and will ultimately help you learn to craft questions that are effective for both you as the researcher and for your readers. Your question(s) should:

- Be answerable with new information (you should not know the answer already)
- Not be a "yes-no" question
- Be broad enough to allow for insights, but narrow enough to be manageable
- Not already be answered by the literature—find your niche in the literature; identify the literature gap or the ambiguity in the literature; consider how you are adding to the professional discourse on the topic
- Show your passion for the topic
- Lead to more questions
- Not be a biased question—i.e., asking "What are the positive effects of . . ." implies there are no negative effects
- Be specific about your research population in your question—i.e., second-grade math students, high school science students, etc.

We hope that this chapter allows you to realize, as Kiyoshi noted, that ideas for writing "'. . . *come from here,' . . . and open[s] his arms wide to take in the river and the sky and the distant buildings. 'And they come from here,' he said, and pointed to his own heart*" (Karlins, 2021, p. 25). But, your head may be spinning, full of ideas, and perhaps wavering between complete commitment to a topic and second-guessing your topic and/or question. That is normal. The reflective activities are here to support you, and it is our belief that by engaging in them you will further explore and understand your next steps toward reaching the potential you are hoping to achieve.

Note. Mandarich, n.d.

⇨ Chapter Two Reflective Activities

Part I: Topic Selection

1. Reflection on Educational History

With a small group of colleagues or classmates, share a bit about your educational history. Think about these questions:

- What led you to become an educator, and what motivates you?

- What experiences, people, and contexts contributed to your perspectives on schooling and education? Tell a story about yourself in the context of schooling that shows something about who you are and how you got here.
- Much is said about what is *wrong* in education today. Describe what you see as the potential in our schools and classrooms. Describe how you see your role in achieving the potential that you have identified.

Following this activity, reflect on how this conversation impacts your ideas for a research topic.

2. Narrowing Your Focus Area of Research

Please use the following questions to help identify an area of research focus:

- What are your core beliefs about the goals, methods, and purpose of education?
- What are the dominant narratives that influence education in your field?
- What are some of the most important contemporary issues in the field, facing educators now?
- What social, cognitive, economic, and political elements impact teaching and learning?
- What are the ramifications of the issues on pedagogy?
- What perspectives (social, cognitive, economic, and political) surround the issues?
- What do you see as the greatest challenge and/or ramification of the issues?
- What is the historical context of each of these current issues?

3. Inside/Outside Circle Activity

In this round-robin sharing, you will be meeting with others in 6-10 minute sessions. The instructor will serve as the timekeeper, giving a signal when the first person should wrap up their discussion and the second person should begin sharing their potential-based research ideas. When signaled, have the outside circle move one chair to the left or right and discuss the same question with a new partner. The goal is for each person to have a chance to talk briefly about their research ideas. As you meet with classmates you may want to take some notes so you remember who you may want to check back in with (sharing articles, discussing, networking with possible connections to research). One of the key objectives of this activity is to allow you to have a chance to talk about your topic as much as possible. Take this as an opportunity to:

- Talk through your ideas
- Gain feedback/brainstorm new ideas
- Talk publicly about your profession
- Glean additional ideas related to your potential-based topic

Enjoy scholarly discussions with peers.

4. Boyer's (1996) Scholarship Reflection

For this activity, you will need to have three research articles connected to your potential research topic. Please read each before continuing through the steps listed below.

Table 2.2 ***Boyer, Reflective Tasks***

Key Word from Boyer et al. (2015)	Definition of Step	Tasks
DISCOVERY	The scholarship of discovery: knowledge acquired through research—"disciplined investigative efforts" (p. 81) in the pursuit of new intellectual knowledge.	• Create a list of key terms from each article and determine at least four overlapping key terms. Use those key terms to find at least one other relevant article. • Review the reference list of each article. Are there references that appear in more than one of your articles? If so, seek out that article as well.

Key Word from Boyer et al. (2015)	Definition of Step	Tasks
SYNTHESIS	The scholarship of integration: knowledge acquired through synthesis—"making connections across the disciplines" (p. 82); serious disciplined work that seeks to interpret, draw together, and bring new insight to bear on original research.	• Using a digital platform or pen and paper, create a visual mind map that shows the interconnections among the articles. (At least the first three and, ideally, others you discovered as part of your initial investigative efforts listed above.)
APPLICATION	The scholarship of application: knowledge acquired through practice—"new intellectual understandings can arise out of the very act of application" (p. 85).	• Hone in on one area of your visual map. Set a timer and brainstorm for at least ten minutes about specific applications for the ideas captured in that section of the mind map. How are these ideas connected to your professional experiences?
TEACHING	The scholarship of teaching: knowledge acquired through teaching—a dynamic endeavor between teachers and learners that increases capacities for reflection, critical and creative thinking, and action.	• With a writing partner, discuss the above steps. Teach each other about the key ideas you have uncovered. Share ideas for action, the reflection you have done since reading the articles, and your ideas for how you would move forward with this topic if you were to choose it as your potential-based area of research.
ENGAGEMENT	The scholarship of engagement: knowledge acquired within any of the above four scholarships through activities that connect the academic with people and places outside the campus and which ultimately direct the work of the academy toward larger, "more humane ends" (p. 127).	• Discipline yourself to take the next four or five days to watch for connections between this potential topic and the world outside the walls of academia. Carry a recording device (phone, notebook) with you at all times and record the real-world connections you discover.

Part II: Developing Research Question(s)

1. Framing your Question(s): What, Why, & How

Complete the "What, Why, & How" chart below for several topic ideas. Doing so will help you begin deciphering which contemporary issue in your field you want to commit your research time to. You may find that doing follow-up charts after your initial topic selection is also helpful. For example, complete the chart; then complete a follow-up chart for a more narrowed topic that surfaced through the additional chart completion for the overarching topic.

Figure 2.1 ***What, Why, & How***

Topic:

<table>
<tr><td>Personal Connections:</td><td>Professional Connections:</td><td>Importance of the Topic:</td></tr>
<tr><td colspan="2">Questions I Have:</td><td>Key Search Terms:</td></tr>
</table>

2. Using AI to Explore Your Research Question(s)

Please use your AI tool of choice to do an initial review of your research topic and question. AI should help to generate new questions, identify key search terms, present multiple/opposing perspectives on your topic, and develop new thinking. For example, after several months of thinking about the topic of potential-based research, we asked Claude AI, our AI tool of choice, to provide possible research questions aligned to this text (see the figure below). Claude provided us with several different ways to explore the issue, as well as introducing us to different disciplines and terminology that expanded our thinking and understanding. We introduce AI as one of many different perspectives on your topic and a potentially helpful tool.

Figure 2.2 ***Asking AI to Brainstorm Research Questions***

Potential-Based Research Questions for a Positive Approach

Can you provide some research questions related to researchers approaching research topics with a potential-based perspective instead of a problem-based perspective?

TH

Here are some potential research questions related to taking a potential-based approach to research topics rather than a problem-based approach:

- How might reframing research around human strengths and capabilities rather than deficits and problems lead to more empowering interventions and policies?
- In what ways could a potential-based perspective allow researchers to identify overlooked assets and resources in communities that could be leveraged?
- What novel insights might emerge by studying instances of human flourishing, resilience, or thriving instead of instances of disorder, distress or dysfunction?
- How might a potential-based approach expand the vision of what's possible and inspire more generative, creative research directions?
- What research methods and tools would best capture a potential-based perspective (e.g. appreciative inquiry, positive deviance, solution-focused approaches)?
- How might funding priorities and structures need to change to support more potential-based research? What barriers currently exist?
- In what ways might a potential-based approach lead to more collaborative, participatory research with communities as co-producers of knowledge?
- What disciplines and fields of research may need to shift to embrace a more potential-based approach? What changes in training are needed?
- How might potential-based research intersect with or contribute to positive psychology, humanistic psychology, capabilities approach, and other strengths-based perspectives?

Let me know if you need any clarification or have additional questions as you develop your research agenda around this topic! I'm happy to discuss further.

A\ Copy Retry

Note. Anthropic, 2024

3. Review of Potential Questions

At this point, you should have a list of potential questions related to potential-based topic(s). Take time to sit with each question and use the following criteria to analyze each. Doing so will allow you to possibly abandon some questions altogether, to refine questions, and to come closer to identifying your strongest question(s). Review of question(s):

- Is your question answerable with data? (It should be answerable.) Do you already know the answer? (If so, you need to find a new question or revise your existing question.)
- Is your question answerable with a "yes-no" response? (Your question should require more than a "yes-no" response.)
- Is your question broad enough to allow for insights, but narrow enough to be manageable?
- Is your question already answered by the literature? Find your niche in the literature; identify the literature gap or the ambiguity in the literature; consider how you are adding to the professional discourse on the topic.
- Does your question reflect your passion for the topic?
- Does your question lead to additional questions?
- Is your question biased? For example, asking, "What are the positive effects of . . ." implies that there are no negative effects.
- Is your question specific to your research population? For example, is your question specific to second-grade math students, high school science students, etc.?

Once you have completed this task on your own, you may also want to use an AI tool of choice to complete a similar analysis of your current research questions.

4. Narrator/Listener Activity

This activity is completed in groups of two. Partners take time sharing and listening during a four-step process in which one person is the narrator and one person is listening and taking notes. The goal is to clarify your research interest.

Step One: The narrator shares their research topic or question as it is currently understood.

Step Two: The narrator tells the story of the topic/question. How and when did the narrator become interested in this topic? How did the interest further develop? Why is this topic compelling?

Step Three: The listener retells the story and checks for understanding of what was said.

Step Four: Use this process to make any revisions to the research question.

(Have partners switch roles as they repeat the process.)

5. Where are you on the Mountain? Assessment of Conditions

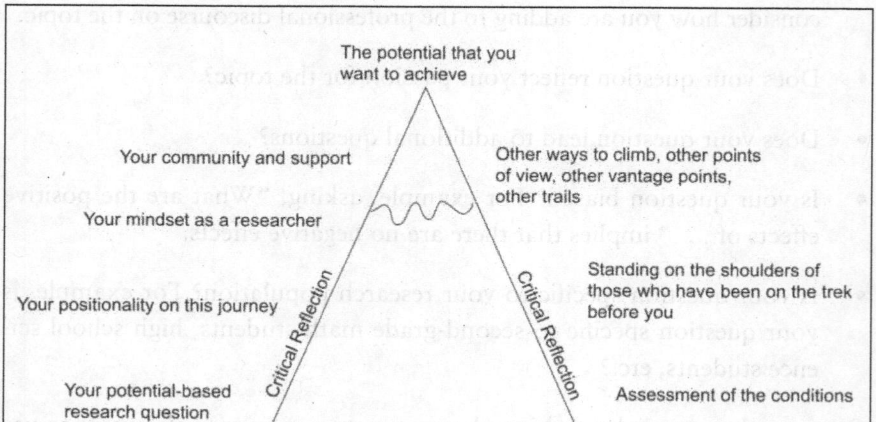

Write a two-page reflection of your current thinking about your potential-based research topic.

As you do this, be sure to:

- Describe the experiences and reasons that draw you to the topic
- Explain the potential that exists in this research area
- Share your research question(s)

References

Anthropic. (2024). *ClaudeAI* (3.5 Sonnet Version) [Large Language Model]. https.//claude.ai/

Block, P. (2003). *The answer to how is yes: Acting on what matters.* Berrett-Koehler Publishers, Inc.

Block, P. (2018). *Community: The structure of belonging* (2nd ed.). Berrett-Koehler Publishers, Inc.

Bochner, A. & Ellis, C. (2016). *Evocative autoethnography: Writing lives and telling stories.* Routledge.

Boyer, E. (1996). The scholarship of engagement. *Journal of Public Service and Outreach, 1*(1), 11–20.

Boyer, E., Moser, D., Ream, T. C., & Braxton, J. M. (2015). *Scholarship reconsidered: Priorities of the professoriate* (Expanded edition.). Jossey-Bass.

Davis, L. P., & Museus, S. D. (2019, July 19). Identifying and disrupting deficit thinking. *Medium.* https://medium.com/national-center-for-institutional-diversity/identifying-and-disrupting-deficit-thinking-cbc6da326995

Dowell, M. -M., Saal, L. K., DiCarlo, C. F., & Willingham, T. D. (2022). *Productivity and publishing: Writing processes for new scholars and researchers.* Sage.

Jane B. (2022, September 14). *Combatting deficit thinking in the classroom.* Teach Simple. https://teachsimple.com/blog/teaching-strategies/deficit-thinking/

Karlins, M. (2021). *Kiyoshi's Walk.* Lee & Low Books.

Mandarich, H. (n.d.). *Keeping your footing on trail* [Photograph]. Unsplash. https://unsplash.com/@hollymandarich

CHAPTER THREE

Who Are You?

I (Trish) started my dissertation work as a white, young new mother in a fairly closeted, long-term committed relationship with my female partner. We had just left the Catholic Church and had found a spiritual community in a Reconciling in Christ Lutheran Church. We had just welcomed a 16-year-old queer Black foster son into our family. Our politics veered way left, and our income was medium (although we were paying out-of-pocket for two EdD degrees). My parents supported and loved me. I had never been part of a supportive LGBTQ+ program as a student or adult. ALL of these factors that amassed into my identity were at play as I started to write my dissertation exploring two LGBTQ+ school support programs for youth.

My identity impacted the 23 interviews that I conducted, transcribed, and analyzed. My identity impacted how I interpreted documents, newspaper articles, and other historical artifacts. Although I wrote my dissertation in the third person and did not include a positionality statement, I was in constant conversation with my dissertation chair about my thoughts and analysis. Was I being objective? Did I correctly interpret the perspective of someone who opposed programming for LGBTQ+ students? Was I too celebratory of folks in my study who were supportive of LGBTQ+ programming? Was I representing both sides equally and objectively? What assumptions did I hold about my topic, my interviewees, and the data that I collected?

The literature in this chapter is designed to help you consider who you are, how your identity impacts your own research, and what steps you can take to be transparent and objective in your work.

Researcher Positionality: Argument and Explanation

We bring our experiences to our work. The background stories shared in Chapter One illustrate that *who we are* impacts what we study, how we design our studies, who we read, who we study, how we analyze our data, and the way we report our findings. Your positionality, or *where you are coming from* (Holmes, 2020), has relevance to the research and should be transparent to the reader; it is a critical component of the Potential-Based Research Framework. For example, as authors of this text, we have underlying beliefs that positionality should be included in a research study. As women with backgrounds in education, women's studies, literature, and political science, *the personal* is part of our professional work and has always been connected. As a member of the LGBTQ+ community (Trish), I bring a different lens to the work; I know I seek the perspectives of historically excluded people when I write, read, or research. And being white women (Trish and Karen), we have a different and more privileged experience than our BIPOC colleagues. This impacts how we interpret events, data, and literature. We are reflective about these experiences when we research, write, present, and work together.

When conducting research, one way to be attentive to the assumptions, experiences, and potential biases that you are bringing to your work is to employ a reflexive approach. Ho and Limpaecher (2022) stated, "The goal of being reflexive is to identify any personal beliefs that may have incidentally affected the research" ("What is Reflexivity?" section). We operate from the belief that researchers do not intentionally create biased studies, but we also employ the belief that an unexamined researcher worldview has the potential to bring bias to the study and that you "as a researcher are obliged to acknowledge the self-interests, values, political ideals, and emotions you bring to your research project" (Bochner & Ellis, 2016, p. 57). Intention and action do not always align, especially without deliberate reflection on the part of the researcher. As Brookfield (1995) noted, "sincerity of their intentions does not guarantee the purity of their practice" (p. 1). You must acknowledge and embrace the fact that your story is not separate from your research.

To address this fact, Mills (2003) encouraged a reflexive approach, defining reflexivity as a self-reflective process to "intentionally reveal underlying assumptions or biases that cause the researcher to formulate a set of questions in a particular way and to present findings in a particular way" (p. 80). Your lived experience has shaped the way that you see the world and the way that you make sense of it. The way we experience the real world is from our own perceptual system that decides what is meaningful, what is real, and what has value (Glasser, 1998). Because of this, two separate researchers are inclined to interpret the same data set in different ways. This does not make the data inaccurate, or the results flawed, and it does not mean that either researcher is "wrong" in their analysis; instead, sharing one's positionality in the interpretation of the research provides a more complete understanding.

With a reflexive approach, you are also bringing an awareness that unexamined research could harm historically marginalized groups. As hooks (1994) reminded us, scholarship and literature can exclude or ignore the experiences of historically marginalized groups, while at the same time making critical arguments and contributions on behalf of the whole. For example, hooks found feminist literature explored the experiences of "women" but only white women. When we share our positionality, we create the space to confront and ask questions such as: Whose voice is missing? What intersectionality is not considered? What privileged insider experience do I bring?

We ask you to question whether or not there is an ethical consideration to sharing your positionality in your research. Research has found that industry-sponsored research tends to be biased in favor of a sponsor's product (Fabbri et al., 2018). Because of this, institutional review boards ask researchers to share if they have received funding to do particular studies. In the same way, if you have had privilege or positive experiences with your research topic *or* if you have experienced inequities or have had negative experiences with your topic, we believe that you should include this as part of your research story.

Note. Rees, 2024

Let's explore an example. If a researcher is looking at the relationship between reading for pleasure at home and reading for achievement in school, the design of the study might be influenced by the researcher's own experiences. What kind of access did the researcher have to books at their home? How was reading prioritized and valued in their family? What type of representation has historically been more present in children and young adult books? (see CCBC, n.d.) How can the researcher be cognizant of how their own journey with reading is impacting how they view the subjects in their study? In another example, a researcher is studying how field trip opportunities impact the eco-literacy of their students. The researcher must consider how their own experiences with field trips and the environment impact the study. Did the researcher have field trip opportunities as a student, and if so, were they positive? Do field trips incur costs for families, and are field trips accessible for all students? Why is eco-literacy important to the researcher, and what politics, values, and beliefs are connected to eco-literacy?

It is valuable to examine these experiences and assumptions. One of the most valuable paradigm shifts that I experienced as a classroom teacher (Trish) was with regard to homework and assumptions that I was making. In my experience as a student, I was able to go home from school and work on homework. If poster board or glue was needed, my parents would run to the store for me. I could spend hours on my homework with no other responsibilities. If I was struggling with a problem or a question, my parents were available to offer their help. There was a desk in my room. If my homework wasn't completed, it was because I was being negligent and/or lazy in getting it done. Because of my personal and privileged experience in this specific area, when I became a teacher, I had a lot of assumptions about missing homework. What I did not realize is that not all students have free nights or the economic means to buy glue, poster board, or markers. I assumed all students had parents or guardians at home helping with their homework. I assumed that missing homework was the result of laziness. At this point in my teaching career, I had to rethink what I was assigning and why. If I were doing research related to homework, these are the assumptions that I would have had to consider. In addition to this review of assumptions in evaluating *who we are*, we must consider the social and political context of our research questions and studies. As a researcher, your values, religious beliefs, politics, social class, gender, sexuality, location, race, ethnicity, and (dis)abilities are at play. We believe that when we consciously and constructively connect *the researcher and the researched* it increases the richness, interconnectedness, and value of our work.

In order to do this transparently, we ask our students to write their culminating projects in the first person. We believe that using first-person language creates a reflective space. Instead of saying "the researcher did this . . ." and "the research found that . . . ," when our students share "I found . . . ," they are conscious of the intersection between who they are and what they found. Ramsey (2005) referred to this as a *narrative-learning cycle* (p. 280), where the researcher can use the reflective process and the re-telling of stories in a transformative inquiry process. More importantly, we also ask our students to state the personal and/or professional "why" that brought them to their work. Whether you are writing your research in the first person or third person, it is valuable to consider and create the space to share this relationship between the researcher and the researched. Making transparent these important connections between experience and the research topic gives the reader a more complete picture and understanding of the work; this purposeful vulnerability on the part of the researcher draws the reader into the research (Adams et al., 2014).

We believe that quantitative, qualitative, and mixed methods approaches all benefit from reflexivity on the part of the researcher. In qualitative research, there is ample agreement in the literature regarding the role of the researcher as a fixed participant of the study. As Bourke (2014) reminded us, "The nature of qualitative research sets the researcher as the data collection instrument" (p. 2). Being considered an instrument in the research process brings a higher level of accountability to your role and position related to the topic. Bukamal (2022) concurred that, "the researcher is an active, not passive, agent in acquiring knowledge" (p. 328). Again, this active role in the qualitative process positions the researcher in a place where their positionality to the topic is a factor of the study. Similarly, Finlay (2002) stated, "As qualitative researchers engaged in contemporary practice, we accept that the researcher is a central figure who influences, if not actively constructs, the collection, selection and interpretation of data" (p. 212). Being transparent and forthcoming about what is impacting how you "influence" and "construct" the study increases the validity of your conclusions.

Reflexivity with quantitative and mixed methods approaches has been infrequently addressed in the literature. Jamieson et al. (2023) acknowledged that quantitative research has "remained seemingly detached from . . . general reflective practice" (p. 2) but argued for the importance of what it offers to quantitative studies. In her discussion of quantitative research in linguistics, Lorette (2023) argued that reflexivity can fill in the "knowledge gaps" that can exist between the data and the context, arguing,

> Reflecting on one's positionality can feel particularly unusual and uncomfortable for quantitative researchers who are supposed to be "absent" from the research outcomes, but doing so enables them to acknowledge their inevitable presence in and impact on the research process and results. (p. 668)

While literature supporting reflexivity with quantitative and mixed methods research is lacking, the existing literature supports a need to acknowledge the relationship between the researcher and the researched.

Literature on a Reflexive Approach in Research

As Glasser (1998) reminded us, our perceived world is always at work in helping us to understand our lived experience. Jacobson and Mustafa (2019) similarly argued, "It is known that the way that researchers perceive the social world is largely dependent on their position within it, which further impacts the way that the research is approached, interacted with, and interpreted" (p. 2). A reflexive approach and the inclusion of the researcher's positionality work to make these perceptions apparent to the reader. Holmes (2020) was especially interested in the impact of a new researcher's positionality, stating, "It is essential for new researchers to acknowledge that their positionality is unique to them and that it can impact all aspects and stages of the research process" (pp. 2–3). Whether you are a new or seasoned researcher, reflexivity is always at play.

This self-understanding begins by acknowledging that "a rigorous researcher can present their findings and interpretations in confidence [because] they have thought about, acknowledged and been honest and explicit about their stance and the influence it has had upon their work" (Sikes, 2004, p. 15). This occurs by being reflexive and reflective. Jamieson et al. (2023) argued that reflexivity is critical but also makes you, as the researcher, vulnerable. If you share only what you want to share, your positionality may not be as honest as it could be.

Through her own research journey using narrative inquiry, Biddings-Muro (2017) reflected, "The dissertation process definitely helped me to refine the process of hearing and listening with intent. My private internal questions had a recurring theme: 'What am I supported to learn from this process?' And 'will I be different when this is all over?'" (p. 167). The process can lead to self-discovery, as it did for Biddings-Muro, in finding her research voice.

Finlay (2002) argued that avoiding reflexivity in research compromises it, but also argued for the need to balance too little and too much. Explaining one's positionality should not be an introspective autobiography where you delve into "the abyss" (Finlay, 2002, p. 227), nor should it be too little where you "dabble near the surface" (p. 227). It should authentically reflect on your own positionality, which Bukamal (2022) identified as multidimensional, including "the researcher's perceived positionality, the researcher's perceived positionality by the research participants, and the researcher's actual positionality" (p. 346). We contend that this multi-faceted, in-depth reflective work that Bukamal identifies is a necessary and productive part of the research process. Your study will be more structurally sound if you identify all of the outside forces that are impacting its design.

There are opponents of reflexivity. They view it as self-indulgent or narcissistic because of the potential to focus on the voice of the researcher instead of the voice of the participants (Finlay, 2002). This criticism reminds us that the researcher's voice and the researcher's experiences should not overshadow the participants' voices and experiences.

We argue that providing transparency with regard to your positionality can reduce potential bias. Additionally, we believe that sharing your connection to the topic illustrates how the researcher and the participants are not separate, but rather, are intertwined. Obviously, participants' voices are essential as they serve as the basis of your findings, but we urge you to have an awareness of the negative and positive power of your own voice within the research and to share that. Indeed, who you are and how each aspect of your mountain is presented within your work is critical. Take time to explore that. Take time to name it. Take time to ensure that it—YOU—are represented in the work because your potential-based work is yours!

⇨ Chapter Three Reflective Activities

1a. Positionality Map

In this activity, the researcher has an opportunity to explore how their positionality intersects with their research topic. The following questions are at the center of this activity: What experiences, biases, or worldview do you bring to your research? How have these been shaped by your politics, ethnicity, race, gender, sexuality, social class, abilities, faith, etc?

Figure 3.1 ***Blank Positionality Map***

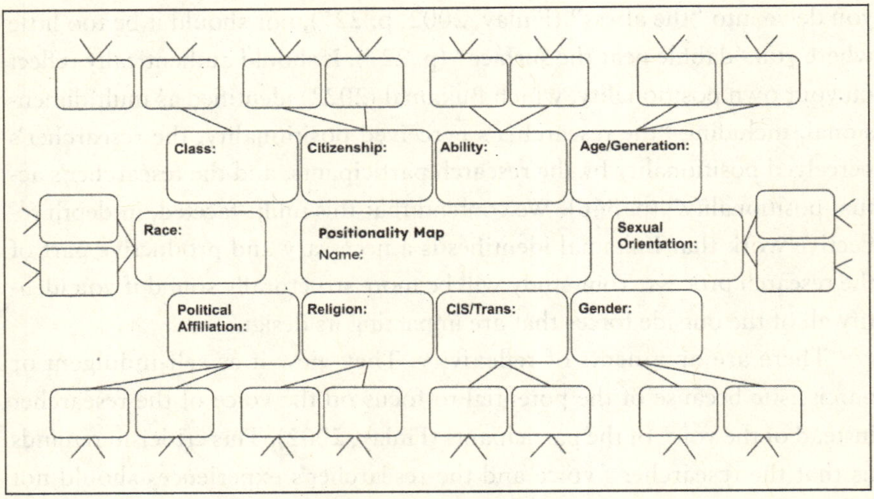

Note. Adapted from Jacobson & Mustafa, 2019, p. 3

1b. Develop a Positionality Statement

Create your own positionality statement using your positionality map from exercise 1a, and considering the quote by Holmes (2020):

> A good strong positionality statement will typically include a description of the researcher's lenses (such as their philosophical, personal, theoretical beliefs and perspective through which they view the research process), potential influences on the research (such as age, political beliefs, social class, race, ethnicity, gender, religious beliefs, previous career), the researcher's chosen or pre-determined position about the participants in the project

Figure 3.2 ***Example of a Completed Positionality Map***

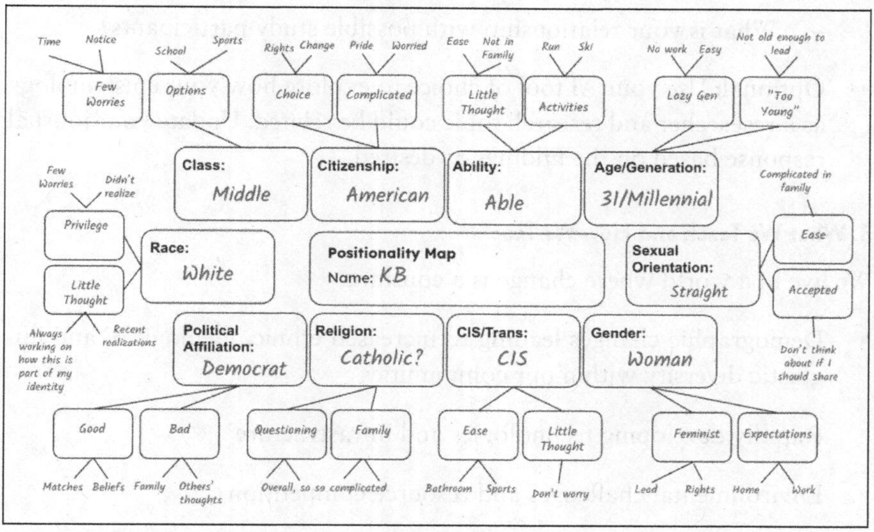

Note. Adapted from Jacobson & Mustafa, 2019, p. 4

(e.g., as an insider or an outsider), the research-project context and an explanation as to how, where, when and in what way these might, may, or have, influenced the research process. (p. 4)

2. Personal Connection Journal Reflection

Complete the following activities individually and be prepared to discuss.

- Take the "What is your epistemology?" (https://www.proprofs.com/quiz-school/story.php?title=epistemology-and-you) online quiz to begin to identify your epistemology. (Note: this is ONE of many tools. Feel free to explore other epistemology identification tools or resources.) Epistemology is the study of knowledge; this quiz attempts to help you understand why you believe what you believe on the epistemology spectrum.
- Write a journal reflection that answers the following:
  - What was the result of the quiz? Do you agree with the results? How does this relate to or inform your research?

  - What is your personal and professional journey with this topic?
  - What is your relationship with possible study participants?
- Optional: Use your AI tool of choice to explore how your epistemology as a researcher and research topic could be related. Update your journal response based on the findings as desired.

3. What We Teach and How We Teach

We live in a world where change is a constant:

- Demographic changes leading to increased ethnic, ideological, and linguistic diversity within our communities
- Rapidly developing technologies and infrastructure
- Environmental challenges and resource competition
- Resource redistribution, economic inequality, new models of school funding
- Changing cultural norms of identity relative to gender, sexuality, race, and ability

If we are to prepare learners to function as productive citizens in these evolving realities, it is vitally important that we begin to unearth the societal norms, values, and ideologies that influence the hidden curriculum.

For this activity:

- Think about how you would describe **what** you do in your educational setting (content, context, skills, attitudes, etc.) as well as **how** you do it.
- Think about how the current individual, local, state, and national contexts influence your understanding of teaching AND learning.

4. Philosophy of Education Activity

Your philosophy is where you will articulate your core beliefs about the goals, methods, and purpose of education (broadly) and how those beliefs are (or will be) integrated with your own practice directly. This will help you organize your working theory of education thus far.

Grounded in the literature that you have reviewed and the conversations you have been involved in, develop a written philosophy that guides your own approach to your research *at this point in time*.

Begin to operationalize your own ideas about your research topic. Be sure to draw from your personal experience and knowledge of teaching and learning as well as the new understandings and ideas generated by other resources.

This activity requires you to think deeply about what has shaped you as an educational leader and to address the following ideas:

- What are your core beliefs about the goals, methods, and purpose of education related to your research topic?
- What are the dominant narratives that influence education in your field as related to your research topic?

5. Progressive Reflections Prompts

In groups of two or three, discuss the following questions:

- What are your first thoughts on a possible research topic? What are you thinking/feeling about the research right now?
- What are your new learnings about the research process? What questions do you have? What are your initial thoughts on a research question?
- Have you made any revisions to your research question(s)? What subtopics will you need to explore to better understand all aspects of your research?
- Have a conversation with a colleague about your research topic. Describe the conversation and what ideas were generated.
- How comfortable are you with the college/university library and its resources? What are your strengths and challenges in gathering research (and writing the literature review)? What questions do you have?
- What are your ideal writing conditions? What is your organizational system for reviewing the literature?

6. Researcher Assumptions

In this activity, list your research topic and consider all the assumptions that you, as the researcher, are bringing to the research.

Researcher Assumption Example:

Topic: Social Presence and Online Learning:

Assumptions:

- Access to technology is pervasive (socioeconomic)
- Social presence is important to learning
- Online learning is a valuable learning environment
- All instructors can improve on social presence, and all instructors want to improve social presence in their courses
- All instructors can teach online
- Relationships matter to all students (regardless of race, gender, sexuality, etc.)

7. Prompts in All Stages of the Research Process

Jamieson et al. (2023) provided a series of reflective prompts for use in all stages of the research process. Build these reflective exercises into each stage of your research.

Figure 3.3 ***Prompt in the Research Process***

Stage of research	Broader reflexivity prompts
Research question and design	• Why do I want to research this group? • To what extent am I "within" the participant group that I am researching? Am I an "insider" or "outsider" researcher (or do I occupy both positions)? • What can I give to this group? Who is represented within the research team?

Stage of research	**Broader reflexivity prompts**
Research question and design	• Should I be the one to research this group, or am I taking space away from someone else?
Data collection	• Am I intruding on this group? How can I make this as non-coercive as possible? • How can I make this research accessible to the population? • Do participants understand what their data will be used for? • Have I thought beyond traditional ethics? Am I acting ethically? • Could my collection methods be problematic?
Data analysis and interpretation	• Am I aware that people have given me this data and that they may not know me (e.g., survey, health, admin data)? • Who are these people behind the data? • If I am using existing datasets, are there any silent assumptions in this dataset? • Could my analysis of the dataset reproduce existing inequalities?
Conclusions and framing	• How does my use of evidence reflect my biases (or the biases of the research team) as researchers and as individuals with their own life, wants, emotions, needs? • What do I gain from this research? What does the population I have studied gain? • Is there a disconnect between the two questions above? If so, consider the first few questions in this table again.

Note. Jamieson et al., 2023, p. 23; licensed under CC-By Attribution 4.0 International

8. Where are you on the Mountain? Assessment of Conditions

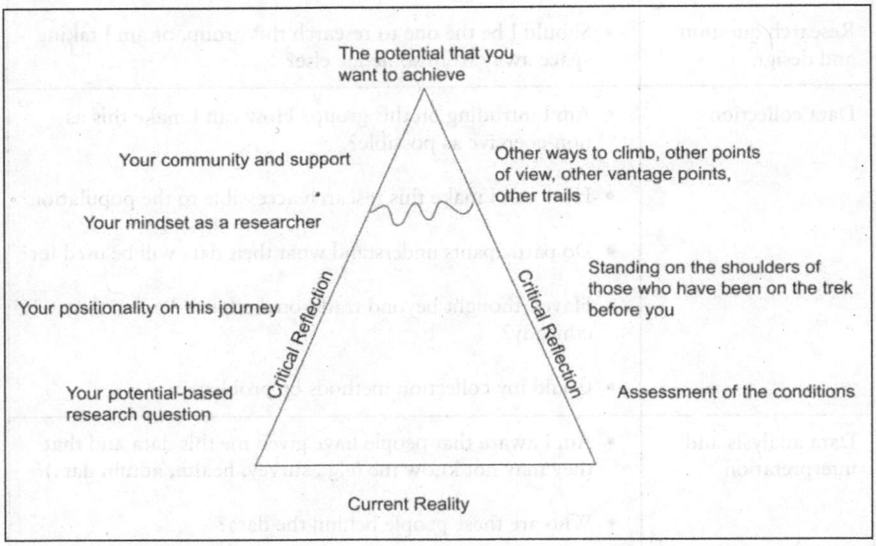

Write a reflection exploring how your positionality and your potential-based research topic are connected.

References

Adams, T., Jones, S. H., & Ellis, C. (2014). *Autoethnography: Understanding qualitative research.* Oxford.

Biddings-Muro, R. (2107). Finding your researcher voice. In *Counterpoints* (Vol. 428), *Outliving your dissertation: A guide for students and faculty* (pp. 165–174). Peter Lang AG. https://www.jstor.org/stable/45177761

Bochner, A., & Ellis, C. (2016). *Evocative autoethnography: Writing lives and telling stories.* Routledge.

Bourke, B. (2014). Positionality: Reflecting on the research process. *The Qualitative Report, 19*(18), 1–9. https://nsuworks.nova.edu/tqr/vol19/iss33/3/

Brookfield, S. D. (1995). *Becoming a critically reflective teacher.* Jossey-Bass.

Bukamal, H. (2022), Deconstructing insider-outsider researcher positionality. *British Journal of Special Education, 49*, 327–349. https://doi.org/10.1111/1467-8578.12426

CCBC. (n.d.) *CCBC Diversity Statistics.* Cooperative Children's Book Center School of Education University of Wisconsin-Madison. https://ccbc.education.wisc.edu/literature-resources/ccbc-diversity-statistics/

Fabbri, A., Lai, A., Grundy, Q., & Bero, L. A. (2018). The influence of industry sponsorship on the research agenda: A scoping review. *American Journal of Public Health, 108*(11), e9–e16. https://doi.org/10.2105/AJPH.2018.304677

Finlay, L. (2002). Negotiating the swamp: The opportunity and challenge of reflexivity in research practice. *Qualitative Research,* 2(2), 209–230. https://doi.org/10.1177/146879410200200205

Glasser, W. (1998). *Choice theory: A new psychology of personal freedom.* HarperCollins.

Ho, L., & Limpaecher, A. (2022). *The importance of reflexivity in qualitative research: Essential guide to coding qualitative data.* Delve. https://delvetool.com/blog/reflexivity

Holmes, A. G. D. (2020). Researcher positionality—A consideration of its influence and place in qualitative research—A new research guide. *International Journal of Education, 8*(4), 1–10. https://files.eric.ed.gov/fulltext/EJ1268044.pdf

hooks, b. (1994). *Teaching to transgress: Education as the practice of freedom.* Routledge.

Jacobson, D., & Mustafa, N. (2019). Social identity map: A reflexivity tool for practicing explicit positionality in critical qualitative research. *International Journal of Qualitative Methods, 18*, 1–12. https://journals.sagepub.com/doi/10.1177/1609406919870075

Jamieson, M. K., Govaart, G. H., & Pownall, M. (2023). Reflexivity in quantitative research: A rationale and beginner's guide. *Social and Personality Psychology Compass, 17*(4), e12735. https://doi.org/10.1111/spc3.12735

Lorette, P. (2023). Opportunities and challenges of positionality in quantitative research: Overcoming linguistic and cultural 'knowledge gaps' thanks to 'knowledgeable collaborators'. *Journal of Multilingual and Multicultural Development*, 44(8), 657–671.

Mills, G. E. (2003). *Action research: A guide for the teacher researcher* (2nd ed.). Merrill Prentice Hall.

Ramsey, C. (2005). Narrating development: Professional practice emerging within stories. *Action Research, 3*(3), 279–295.

Rees, L. (2024, April 24). *Best Pyrenees trekking: Top 5 long-distance Pyrenean treks* [Photograph]. Awe365.com. https://awe365.com/best-pyrenees-trekking-top-5-long-distance-pyrenean-treks/

Sikes, P. (2004). Methodology, procedures, and ethical concerns. In C. Opie (Ed.), *Doing educational research: A guide for first time researchers* (pp. 15–33). Sag

CHAPTER FOUR

Embracing a Mindset of Inquiry

In this short but powerful book, author Kobi Yamada (2014) walks readers through the journey of having an idea, an idea that may feel "strange and fragile," and what we can do to embrace, nurture, and ultimately share that idea with others. Often, as shared in the book, we as researchers and writers have ideas but question whether they are worthy of exploration. We walk away from them or keep them to ourselves. The ideal potential-based topics, though, stick with us, and they move, as Yamada (2014) says, "from being here to being everywhere . . . a part of everything" (p. 31). We encourage you to read this short picture book and to overlay it with your mindset about research and writing. As shared in Chapter Two, ideas are all around us. We encourage you to use What Do You Do With an Idea? *as a visual reminder that your ideas can grow and, through your full engagement, as explored through this text's reflective activities, can become part of your daily thoughts. Those ideas can and need to be shared.*

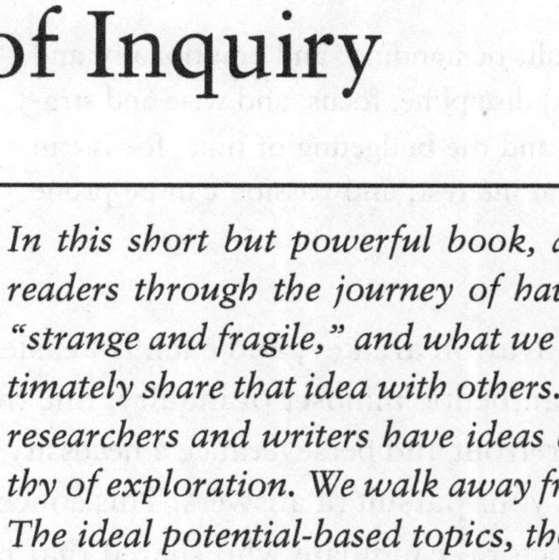

Note. Yamada, 2014

Embracing a Mindset of Inquiry: Argument and Explanation

Trust your ideas, trust yourself, and know that with a strong potential-based topic identified and a solid question that will drive your work, you are well on your way to completing a successful research project. It is a project, however, and projects take time, discipline, and motivation. As Dowell et al. (2022) stated,

> Scholarly, academic writing is difficult, demanding, and emotionally and physically draining work. It require[s] discipline, focus, and wise and strategic use of time. Without discipline and the budgeting of time, focus can be hard to maintain. Choice, personal interest, and passion can be prime motivators when writing. (p. 8)

Indeed, time, discipline, and motivation are key, and each is "easier" to achieve if you have or develop an authentic mindset of inquiry, one that keeps curiosity and potential at the forefront and perseverance a necessity as you push through obstacles and relish your pursuit of answers. This concept was clear in a conversation with a doctoral candidate who shared that her research was motivating to her because the knowledge she was gaining was "[becoming] part of [her] moving forward not 'just' because of the end product but because it [was] important to [her] work as an educator; it [was] changing [her] as a person" (S. Lee, personal communication, May 12, 2023). This motivation drives us, but that is not to say that we will not encounter times when we feel unmotivated or begin to question whether we are really up to the task of sharing our ideas with others. With those hurdles in mind, within this chapter, we explore theories related to mindsets and discuss what we believe are necessary frameworks as one works to find their place in the research: constructivism and inquiry.

Literature on the Mindset of a Researcher

First, we explore the overarching concept of *mindset* which Wilhelm (2009), paraphrasing various authors, described as "the willingness and capacity to try on alternate ways of thinking and being and practicing, the consciously taken responsibility for inquiry (open-minded exploration, data-driven decisions, disciplinary ways of thinking—both for students and teachers), and a wide-awake reflectivity and reflexivity" (p. 36). As a wide-awake educational researcher, it is essential that you create a mindset that moves beyond digging into the research of others and determining how that research applies to your own setting to one where you employ a constructivist approach where you explore "both what 'knowing' is and how one 'comes to know'" (Fosnot, 2005, p. ix). With this type of mindset you are able to look at your potential-based research topic in a manner that allows you to, as Brooks and Brooks (1999) stated, " [make] sense of our world by synthesizing new experiences into what [you] have previously come to understand" (p. 4). When you bring this constructivist approach to your research, it allows you to connect with your topic in ways that fuel your passion.

This synthesis of experiences ultimately is the foundation for inquiry that then propels your research as you work to fully understand the phenomena involved in those experiences.

> Teacher inquiry simply means using . . . the "tomorrow mind" instead of the "yesterday mind," that is, adopting . . . a welcoming attitude to change, thus activating the problem-solving mind in favor of the status quo mind. Teacher-researchers see the classroom as a rich set of data that can be used to learn how to teach better and to inform the changes they are committed to making. (Wilhelm, 2009, p. 38)

Experience inspires and challenges action researchers who develop ideas based on their work in an educational setting and use their research, as Stringer and Aragón (2021) stated, "not just to gain knowledge but to put the knowledge emerging from the research to practical use" (p. xviii). This definition of inquiry clearly aligns with our focus on potential-based rather than problem-based research and reminds us that, as Wilhelm (2009) stated, "If we want to work toward any of our goals as educators, we must be willing to try innovative . . . constructive ways of teaching . . . and we must reflect on and be willing to share what happens as a result" (p. 36). Coming to a topic that you are passionate about, researching it, and sharing results with others help to perpetuate an inquiry mindset, as these activities constantly remind you of your purpose and the topic's relevancy.

Note. Freerange Stock, 2024

Transitioning from a Problem-Based to a Potential-Based Mindset

In environments where Problem-Based-Learning (PBL) methods are used, Hung (2011) stated, "students' learning is initiated and consequently driven by a need to solve an authentic . . . real-world problem" (p. 531). Indeed, the way a researcher approaches a project, their mindset, is critical. The energy one is able to give to the project propels it forward. The reality, though, is that we are humans, and doubt, fear, and/or apathy will creep in; we will fall back to a problem-based mindset if we do not consciously remind ourselves to focus on the potential that exists.

It is essential, then, that you look at your core beliefs about a given "problem" and give time and space to the noodling that needs to occur in order for passion to be built in an authentic and meaningful manner that mandates you as a researcher to take action with potential always at the forefront. Stringer and Aragón (2021) discussed this need to give ideas and yourself the space and time needed to have a mindset of possibilities as they discussed the importance of "approach[ing] capacity-building spaces . . . more slowly and emergently, engaging in more open questioning, reflection, active listening, and systematic documentation of the active stories in the room" (p. xix). Through this intentional process of allowing your ideas to more fully develop, and with a strong belief in the need to take action, your mindset will naturally lean toward the belief that "solutions" need to be found and shared and that YOU are just the person to do so.

Accepting and Conquering the Impostor Phenomenon

Shifting one's self-perception of who they are as a professional to include the terms "researcher" and "scholar" is exciting but usually also brings a level of self-doubt as one reflects on their current practice(s) and their ability to make change. When you do this reflective work, you might question yourself and your own abilities. This is natural, as was shared by Clance and Imes (1978) when they first coined the term *impostor syndrome* which they described as a psychological experience of intellectual and professional fraudulence. When exploring this concept, Josa (2022) shared the four P indicators of impostor syndrome—perfectionism, paralysis, people-pleasing, and procrastination. In our work with doctoral students, we have had students who exhibit one or more of these deterrents. For example, some feel they cannot move forward because they expect perfection in first drafts; some experience paralysis when obstacles enter their pathway; some apologize to us around their feelings of inadequacy and/or select topics that they think they should research; and some students procrastinate to the point of stalling out of the process. Realistically, you as the writer may experience each of these individually or collectively as you navigate through the process of selecting, researching, and writing about your potential-based topic.

It is natural to experience impostor syndrome during the process, but through effective topic selection, concrete planning, and perseverance, you will consistently be able to shift from being uncertain to confident. In our work with graduate students, we provide several "first dates" between researchers and their research topics. These small, reflective assignments help to ensure that the researcher's passion and interest in the research topic are long-lasting. Compatibility is a must in the long process of dissertation research and also helps to increase your confidence in your topic selection. We have found that confidence also improves with a potential-based approach; it is motivating and inspiring to work toward a potential-based research goal. Our hope is that this motivation and inspiration work to combat impostor syndrome.

Another way to overcome impostor syndrome will happen naturally as you read literature and enter into the academic conversation on your research topic. Knowing the vocabulary, understanding the arguments, being able to speak the jargon, expanding your ways of understanding the topic, and allowing definitions to become part of your vernacular will dissipate the "phony" (Clance & Imes, 1978, p. 241), fraudulent, and inferior feelings referenced by Clance and Imes.

Within this chapter and specifically through the suggested reflective activities below, it is our hope that you are able to master academic writing through personal discipline and a keen focus on the process which ultimately leads to a stronger end product. Having concrete structures in place will allow you to push through when feelings of being an impostor begin to stifle your ability to move forward.

⇨ Chapter Four Reflective Activities

1. Impostor Phenomenon Assessment

Complete the Clance IP Scale (https://paulineroseclance.com/pdf/IPTestandscoring.pdf) (Clance, 1985) individually. We encourage you to then talk to a trusted colleague, classmate, or personal contact using the following as a guide:

- What was the result?
- Do you agree with the results?
- How does this relate to or inform your work as a writer and researcher?

2. What Do You Do With an Idea?

As you read the picture book, *What Do You Do With an Idea* (Yamada, 2014), stop at each page to think about how the specific visuals and text connect to each stage of your own journey with your chosen topic. How does each stage support your mindset of inquiry (or inhibit it)?

3. How We Tell Stories

Read each of the following quotes. Select one and reflect on the "story" related to your research topic. What is your role in telling the story? How does your researcher mindset come into play when telling this story?

> If stories come to you, care for them. And learn to give them away where they are needed. . . . Sometimes a person needs a story more than food to stay alive. That is why we put these stories in each other's memories. This is how people care for themselves.—Barry Lopez, *The Crow and the Weasel* (as cited in Knight, 2013, p. 175)

> At its best, a story provides an audience with insight into the tacit dimensions of whatever is being discussed. [It] provides context for understanding. A story conveys emotion, humor, and humanity. In short, to hear an effective story is to be reminded that we are alive, sharing the world with other people who know and have experienced events similar to those that make up our own lives. (Knight, 2013, p. 189)

4. Overcoming Deficit Thinking

Using the following prompts, dialogue with a peer to find your strengths as a researcher:

- Starting with your research topic:
  - Share your strengths as related to the topic. Share five things that you could already teach someone else in relation to your research topic.
  - Discuss possible assumptions that others might make about your topic. Discuss the impact of these assumptions and why they must be challenged.
  - Consider how the dominant system creates pressure, barriers, or harm as related to your research topic. Consider the core principles/systems related to your research topic.

(Adapted from Albers, 2013; Jane B., 2022; Plotinsky, 2023)

5. Researcher Identity Memo

Please complete the activity below.

Figure 4.1 *Researcher Identity Memo*

Researcher Identity Memo: The purpose of this memo is to help you examine your goals, experiences, assumptions, feelings, and values as they relate to your research, and to help you discover what resources and potential concerns your identity and experience may create. What prior connections (social and intellectual) do you have to the topics, people, or settings you plan to study? How do you think and feel about these topics, people, or settings? What assumptions are you making, consciously or unconsciously, about these? What do you want to accomplish or learn by doing this study?

The purpose is *not* to write a *general* account of your goals, background, and experiences. Instead, describe specifically those experiences, and the beliefs, goals, and expectations that emerged from them, that are most directly relevant to your planned research project so that you can reflect on *how* these have informed and influenced your research.

The memo is intended to be mainly for your benefit, not for communicating to someone else. For this memo, reflection and analysis are more important than presentation. I suggest that you begin working on this memo by brainstorming whatever comes to mind when you think about your prior experiences that may be related to your site or topic, and jot these down without immediately trying to organize or analyze them. Then, try to identify the issues most likely to be important in your research, think about the implications of these, and organize your reflections. Next are broad sets of questions that are productive to reflect on in this memo. In your answers, try to be as specific as you can.

1. What prior experiences have you had that are relevant to your topic or setting? What beliefs and assumptions about your topic or setting have resulted from these experiences? What goals have emerged from these, or have otherwise become important for your research? How have these experiences, assumptions, and goals shaped your decision to choose this topic, and the way you are approaching this project?
2. What potential advantages do you think the goals, beliefs, and experiences that you described have for your study? What potential disadvantages do you think these may create for you, and how might you deal with these?

Note. Adapted and used with permission, Maxwell, 2013, pp. 34–35

6. Where are you on the mountain? Assessment of Conditions

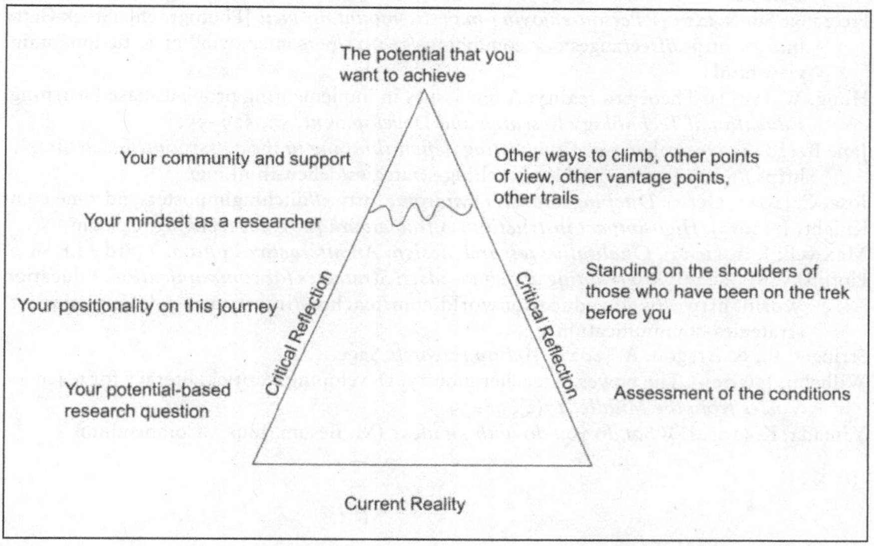

Write a reflection of your current thinking about your potential-based research topic.

- Describe your mindset as a researcher.
- Explore any times in your professional life that you have encountered impostor syndrome. Explain the circumstances and how you prevailed.

References

Albers, R. (2013, April 2). *Tools for teaching: Ditching the deficit model.* Edutopia. https://www.edutopia.org/blog/teaching-tool-ditching-deficit-model-rebecca-alber#:~:text=Ask%20students%20to%20list%20what,grow%20and%20accomplish%20these%20goals

Brooks, J., & Brooks, M. (1999). *In search of understanding: The case for constructivist classrooms.* Association for Supervision and Curriculum Design.

Clance, P. R. (1985). *The impostor phenomenon: When success makes you feel like a fake.* Bantam Books.

Clance, P. R., & Imes, S. A. (1978). The impostor phenomenon in high achieving women: Dynamics and therapeutic interventions. *Psychotherapy: Theory Research and Practice, 15*, 241–247.

Dowell, M.-M., Saal, L. K., DiCarlo, C. F., & Willingham, T. D. (2022). *Productivity and publishing: Writing processes for new scholars and researchers.* Sage.

Fosnot, C. (2005). *Constructivism: Theory, perspectives, and practice* (2nd ed.). Teachers College.

Freerange Stock. (2024). *Person-enjoying-majestic-mountain-view* [Photograph]. iStock Getty Images. https://freerangestock.com/photos/163811/person-enjoying-majestic-mountain-view.html

Hung, W. (2011). Theory to reality: A few issues in implementing problem-based learning. *Educational Technology Research and Development, 59*, 529–552.

Jane B. (2022, September 14). *Combatting deficit thinking in the classroom*. Teach Simple. https://teachsimple.com/blog/teaching-strategies/deficit-thinking/

Josa, C. (2022, Oct 4). *Ditching imposter syndrome*. https://ditchingimpostersyndrome.com/

Knight, J. (2013). *High-impact instruction: A framework for great teaching*. Corwin.

Maxwell, J. A. (2013). *Qualitative research design: An interactive approach* (3rd ed.). Sage.

Plotinsky, M. (2023). *Interrupting deficit mindset: Strategies for communication*. Education World. https://www.educationworld.com/teachers/interrupting-deficit-mindset-strategies-communication

Stringer, E., & Aragón, A. (2021). *Action research*. Sage.

Wilhelm, J. (2009). The power of teacher inquiry: Developing a critical literacy for teachers. *Voices from the Middle, 17*(2), 36–39.

Yamada, K. (2014). *What do you do with an idea?* (M. Besom, Illus.). Compendium.

CHAPTER FIVE

Your Community and Your Support

We ask students to create writing groups to support one another during the dissertation phase of the doctoral program. One of the most successful writing groups, in terms of completing their dissertations in a timely manner, was comprised of three women and one man—one school administrator, two classroom teachers, and one person working for a non-profit organization. Their relationships traversed personal and professional domains; they ended up being friends and colleagues. They formed their writing group early in the program, worked closely during topic selection, and supported one another during the peaks/valleys of the writing process. They met every week, either by phone, in-person, or virtually, on Monday nights. When one person finished their dissertation, they all attended the defense and held a celebration afterward. Even as members finished, they continued to meet, and those that had finished provided feedback and/or did other work. All group members finished in less than two years. Having a community of support might be the most important factor in your research journey!

Professional Community: Argument and Explanation

In completing your research study, surrounding yourself with a support team is a key ingredient for being successful (and finishing). While the make-up of each person's support team will differ, we recommend that your community of support include individuals from three key areas of your life—professional, co-learners in your program, and personal. Having members from each of these areas is beneficial, as each area of your life contributes differently to your motivation, your processing of the content, and your ability to complete a research project. Circling yourself with a support team from each of these areas ensures that your potential-based topic and your progress toward research completion are never far from your mind. People will ask you about it; people will push you when needed; and people will make you go take a walk with them to keep a realistic balance. It is important to talk about your research *as much* and *as often* as you can, and members from each different area of your life can support this in different ways because as Kvam (2018) poignantly stated, "Discussion itself can help to change the boundaries of [ideas]" (p. 710). How you engage in dialogue with each member of your support team and what you ask of each person and the group as a whole will vary. In your professional setting that most aligns with the area of research you are pursuing, you will be able to use professional jargon; those listening will know the key stakeholders and dynamics at play, and be able to nurture your thinking through that understanding. Your co-learners in your program will be able to support you as you discuss your research process. Even if your co-learners are not aligned with your specific topic or setting, they are intimately aware of the research process and the demands of completing a study of this magnitude. Finally, members of your personal support team are also able to listen and able to provide an "outsiders' take" on your topic by asking clarifying questions that you may then want to further explain or explore within your research. There is also value in needing to explain your potential-based topic to those not in your field of study because this forces you as the writer and researcher to explain the issue and process in a simplified manner verbally, and often then, within the context of the final product.

Lean on the community provided by the support team you create, but know in advance that there will more than likely be times that some individuals show research conversation fatigue. This is natural. The topic you are exploring has become part of who you are; it does not need to take on this all-encompassing nature for your community of support. Allow your community of support to provide tough love. Allow them to talk through your ideas and offer suggestions. Allow them to be there and (at times) to not be there, but please remember that ultimately it is YOU who will need to take charge of your topic and write.

Note. Cain, 2016

Literature on Your Community and Your Support

Our professional experience provides solid evidence of the importance of creating a community of support. The research literature provides similar evidence. Bransford and Moroz (2020) addressed the importance of professional support and shared the following foundational components that need to be established for learning communities to thrive:

> **Foundational Component 1:** Create safe academic space
>
> **Foundational Component 2:** Establish and act upon collective and personal purposes and goals
>
> **Foundational Component 3:** Embrace a community of equal partners
>
> **Foundational Component 4:** Establish and enhance connectedness (pp. 404–405)

While the list above addresses components of successful learning communities, we believe these components also apply to successful communities of support. In particular, Foundational Components 1 and 4 become critical, encouraging you to seek out those who will be willing to be your safe space for deep conversation and suggesting that you work to heighten the connections with these individuals. Doing so will allow these members to fully support you as you work through research and the dissemination of findings related to your potential-based research topic. The safe space for conversation and connectedness will also allow you to probe your community of support in ways that heighten your understanding of the topic you are exploring. Therefore, as you work to identify your community of support, we encourage you to ask, as Bransford and Moroz (2020) recommended, if there are "dispositions and/or background experiences that need to be acknowledged and/or emphasized [related to each member of your community] to successfully create an academic space where the complex issues can be explored" (p. 406). Doing so allows you to be pushed by others and to intentionally seek out what you can learn from others as you "focus on your professional goals, taking risks in an environment free of judgment" (Bransford & Moroz, 2020, p. 414). This level of risk-taking as you explore your topic more deeply with others requires an "intentionality of getting to know each other . . . and being willing . . . to consider accepting constructive feedback from [others]" (Bransford & Moroz, 2020, p. 414).

Not only does this support help you in the selection of a topic, but it also pushes you to deepen your understanding of the potential that exists with your topic. As Vygotsky (1978) reminded us, social interaction in the development of knowledge and co-construction of knowledge are central to making meaning in the individual and in the community as a whole. For many, this is a paradigm shift in how we think about education and the research process—moving from an individual experience to an experience that engages and involves others, resulting in a bond that extends learning (Moroz et al., 2022, p. 29). That extension of learning is amplified when you intentionally create a community of support that includes individuals in your professional community, co-learners in your program, and people in your personal circles.

Who is Your Community of Support?

There are three communities of support that we will discuss, including the community in your professional setting, the community related to your graduate work, and your personal community. All three are equally important to you as you take your research journey; all three play an active role as you decide on an area of research focus.

Your Professional Setting

You "live" in your work world. The people you are surrounded by in your professional setting become your friends and your trusted partners in doing the challenging and exciting work asked of educators. It is essential that you engage in dialogue with colleagues because as Kvam (2018) stated, "Raising issues with each other also provides the right conditions for being able to reformulate, adjust and develop opinions about teaching practice" (p. 434). Ideally, this is something that you have already normalized in your professional setting and something that you can rely on as you continue to explore your potential-based ideas for research.

With the work you have accomplished thus far, you are now ready to take your three or four topics to the teacher's lounge or wherever your professional conversations take place. It is time to talk through them with a wide variety of colleagues in an attempt to determine what resonates with others and what "feels right" when you are explaining it. This notion of how discussion can deepen understanding and provide new avenues of thought was addressed by Piaget (1964). He was concerned with how knowledge is developed and believed that dialogue between educators encourages questioning of existing ideas and "can trigger situations where teachers discover that earlier understandings do not concur with new experiences, perceptions and observations [that] stimulate accommodation processes, a change in the schema and hence also new understanding" (Piaget, 1964, p. 700). Through these conversations and new understandings, motivation, both for you and for those you are talking to, should be fostered, because the more your research helps your community, the more motivated you will be to get it done. Through deepened conversation, you will gain a sense of responsibility to complete your research and writing project so that your community will benefit from your end results.

When thinking about how to expand your professional community beyond your work environment, you are encouraged to reach out to scholars in your field of study (see Chapter Seven). They will share your passion for the topic and have a wealth of knowledge. Some of our graduate students are intimidated by the thought of engaging with well-known scholars in their field, but typically, these scholars find it rewarding to discuss their research. They can help to identify gaps in the research as you consider your own specific focus.

In conclusion, as you engage with those in your professional community, you should keep in the back of your mind the possibility of eventually having them serve on your dissertation committee. You can use these conversations in your professional community as a way to "interview" potential committee members.

Note. Photograph taken by author, Harvey (2024).

Your Program—Cohort and Community

Those in your academic program, including fellow students and faculty, are key to your success because they understand your end goal; they become a source of accountability. It is our hope that through the course of your program, you are able to thrive alongside classmates as committed as you are, and that through well-designed interactive experiences, you have opportunities to co-construct knowledge, which Vygotsky (1978) asserted is central to making meaning. As researchers who are seeking to better understand their potential-based topics, learning to relish this process of co-constructing knowledge is essential, as it "provides scholars with constructive feedback as well as a social forum for academic[s] to both connect and collaborate" (Dowell et al., 2022, p. 11). This ability to connect and collaborate is critical, as evidenced in the quote below from a case study of a 20-year-old doctoral program:

> Dissertation writing can feel lonely and unending, but a great way to keep your bearings is to be a part of . . . a group of people who will hold you accountable for progress, whether online or in person. Share your goals and what you are working on with your group, keep track of your progress, and celebrate the work you have done. (Goodman Chien, 2023, p. 195).

Within your group, dialogue will become a constant—one that serves as a source of feedback and inspiration as you continue to explore your potential-based topic. Through dialogue with your learning peers, your understanding of your topic will be enhanced, as indeed, "dialogue is one of the simplest ways we can begin as teachers, scholars, and critical thinkers to cross boundaries, the barriers that may or may not be erected by race, gender, class, professional standing, and a host of other differences" (hooks, 1994, p. 130). Dialogue deepens your understanding and allows you to look at your topic through different lenses based on varied lived experiences. In addition to these peer-to-peer conversations, remember that part of your faculty's experiences include assisting many others in developing strong potential-based topics. Lean on them, as dialoguing with them provides another opportunity to talk about your topic and to benefit from their experience in the field.

Dowell et al. (2022) reminded us, "Having supportive others . . . will propel you forward in your publishing and productivity goals because these individuals can and should serve as critical friends. Your collaborative relationships . . . offer you critical feedback on . . . your arguments" (p. 194). The more you engage in conversation with classmates and faculty members, the more you will gain valuable feedback on your topic.

Personal Community

The final group of people that is critical to include in your community of support consists of those in your personal life whose support you have had and that you will need as you move through the research process. One might think that we are highlighting this part of your community of support because these will be the people that literally help you through your degree as they step in with childcare, encouragement, and an "escape" from the hard work of completing a major writing task by maintaining routines and traditions that have always been important to you. Those roles are important, and their value certainly should not be minimized, but here we want to remind you that these people also can serve a critical role in deepening your understanding of and ability to work toward the top of the potential-based mountain. They do so in some key ways.

First, those in your personal life have more than likely been with you on your journey for longer than those in your workplace or your classmates. They have witnessed how your personal and your professional lives have intersected and, as a result, they may have perspectives that others do not. In describing your potential-based research to them, these members of your community of support may be able to connect your present research back to an earlier work or personal experience. They may remind you of a time that you had forgotten and help you make a connection with that past experience to your current work. Their ability to walk down memory lane with you is something that can highlight stops along your professional journey that have led you where you are today. Analyzing those experiences and how they are potentially present in your current research can push thinking in new directions.

Also of importance is the "hard love" that personal relationships afford us. For many, those in our personal circle are able to do and say things in ways that those in our professional circles cannot. Strong professional relationships are a gift, but few allow us to fully be our complete vulnerable selves, and few move beyond communication and actions that follow certain written or unwritten "norms" about how colleagues interact. Identifying people in your life who are able to play a *personal* role in your larger community of support ensures that you have people you can talk through ideas with who may be able to respond in a way that jars you but ultimately could push your thinking.

We have also experienced ourselves and witnessed in our students the value of discussing our potential-based topics with personal community of support members who are in a different line of work. Describing a topic or research question in a manner that is understandable to someone not steeped in the jargon and nuances of your career is hard, but doing so often "takes you back to the basics" and allows you to uncover different ways to explain or further understand the topic. These social interactions centered around your research with people who are not deeply entrenched in your day-to-day work or the learning you are doing in your program will often include questions or statements from them such as, "I don't get why . . .;" "have you ever thought of . . .;" or "at my work we. . . ." At the time they are uttered, these questions and statements may feel annoyingly abrasive, but we encourage you to embrace them. They serve a strong purpose: They help you think outside the traditional educational ways of approaching situations. They push you to clearly explain why the topic you have chosen is important and to clearly identify its purpose and potential.

The reflective activities shared next will serve as a guide as you work to create your community of support. With this community of support in place, you will reap the benefits noted in the book, *Better Together* (Putnam & Feldstein, 2004), in which "Putnam and co-author Lewis M. Feldstein explain that '*social capital*' refers to social networks, norms of reciprocity, mutual assistance, and trustworthiness. The central insight of this approach is that social networks have real value both for the people in those networks . . . as well as for the bystanders" (as cited in Block, 2018, p. 18).

⇨ Chapter Five Reflective Activities

1a. Reflect on your Professional Community

In your journal, please respond to the following prompts:

- Who are my distant mentors or mentors-on-the-page whose work can help me frame the issues I am most interested in? (Dowell et al., 2022, p. 11)
- Brainstorm a list of all the different professional communities of which you are a part.
- Within those communities, identify the individuals who can serve as members of your professional community and explain the perspectives, experiences, dispositions, expertise, etc., that will increase the quality of

your research and expand your thinking. Consider where each individual exists within the identified rings in the figure below.

Figure 5.1 *Professional Community Rings*

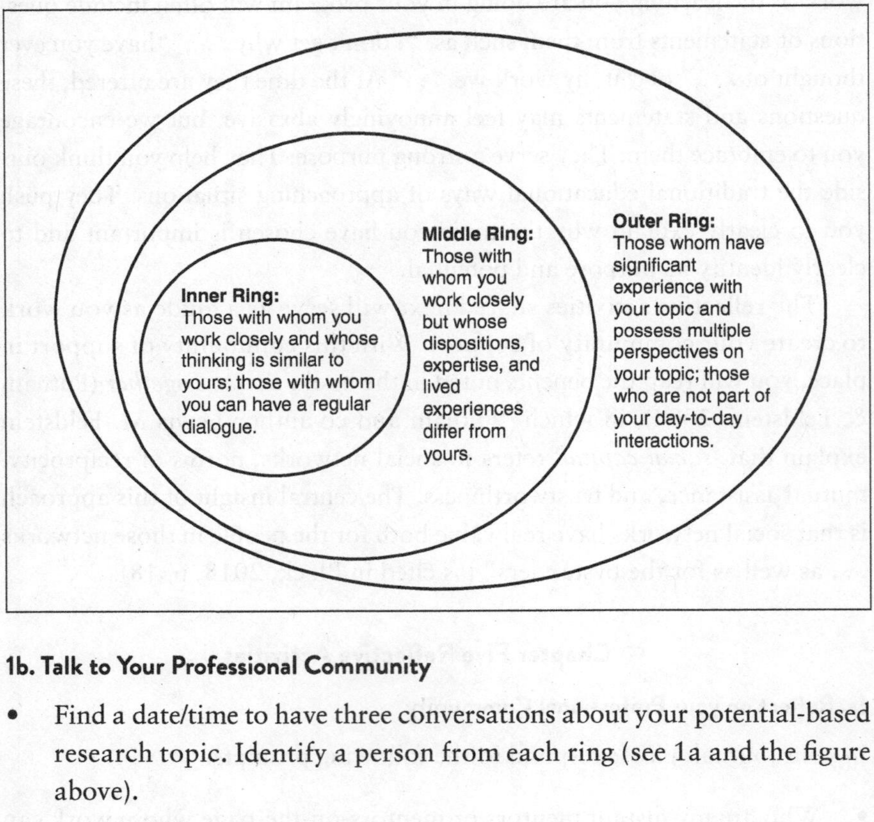

1b. Talk to Your Professional Community

- Find a date/time to have three conversations about your potential-based research topic. Identify a person from each ring (see 1a and the figure above).
  - Explain what potential-based research is.
  - Discuss your topic and lean into insights, feedback, and ideas.
- Capture these discussions in a one- or two-page reflection.

2. Reflect on your Community of Learners in your Program

- Repeat Part 1, Activity 3: **Inside/Outside Circle Activity**, from Chapter Two, with a new focus: In this round-robin sharing, you will be meeting with others in 6-10 minute sessions. The instructor will serve as the timekeeper giving a signal when the first person should wrap up their discussion and the second person should begin sharing their potential-based research ideas. When signaled, have the outside circle move one chair to the left or right and discuss the same question with a new partner. As you meet with classmates you may want to take some notes so you remember who you may want to check back in with (about shared articles, for discussion, or for networking with possible connections to research). One of the key objectives of doing this exercise at this stage of the process is to allow you to hear varied perspectives on your topic. Take this as an opportunity to:

- Talk through your potential-based topic
- Elicit feedback and perspective from your classmates
- Consider which classmates might be a good fit for a writing group for support and accountability

- Schedule a time to meet with a faculty member. Be prepared to discuss your topic and to create a list of possible next steps based on their feedback.

3. Reflect on Your Personal Community

Have a discussion with someone in your personal community who has the least background knowledge and understanding about your topic (but will be a good listener and questioner). Explain your potential-based research topic with as many details as possible. First, listen closely to how YOU are explaining your topic; this may give you additional insight about your purpose in doing the research. Second, listen closely to their questions—you may not have answers for every question, but record them to consider later.

4. Technology as Part of Your Community

Consider the role of technology as part of your community of support. How can AI tools help in developing your thinking and wording, and in formulating your topic? Write a short reflection.

5. Where Are You on the Mountain? Assessment of Conditions

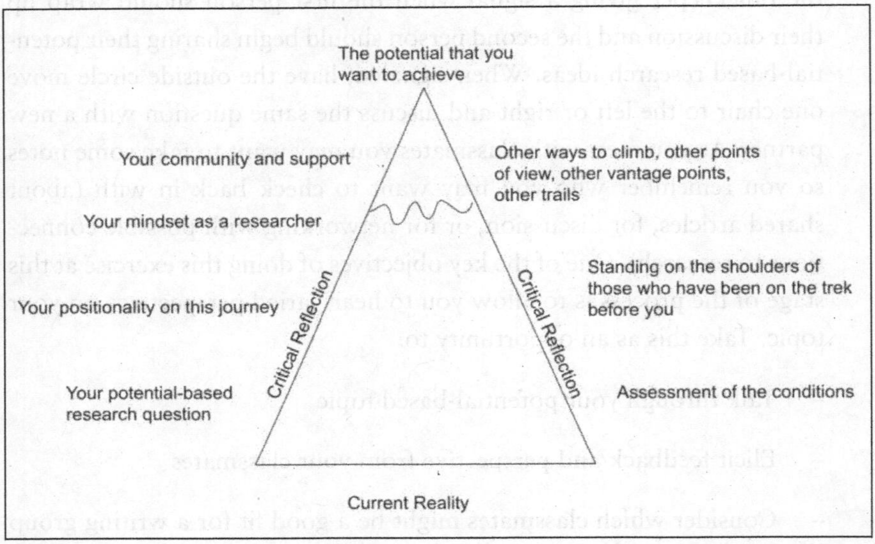

Write a short reflection: Through the above activities, you started to identify and nurture your community of support; you may have also identified areas where you do not have sufficient support. In the case of the latter, strategize how you will work to fill gaps. As you continue to climb, lean on the people in your support community and also be ready to welcome new "hikers" to join you, as the more you delve into your topic, the more you will notice others with whom you would benefit from talking.

References

Block, P. (2018). *Community: The structure of belonging* (2nd ed.). Berrett-Koehler Publishers, Inc.

Bransford, K., & Moroz, K. (2020). A decade of thriving: Learning from one faculty learning community's success. In A. Schwartz, & R. L. Miller (Eds.), *High impact educational practices: A review of best practices with illustrative examples* (pp. 403–416). Society of the Teaching of Psychology.

Cain, K. (2016). *Along the Ridge Trail on Old Rag Mountain* [Photograph]. Wikipedia Commons. https://commons.wikimedia.org/wiki/File:Lending_a_Hand..._(27707003493).jpg

Dowell, M.-M., Saal, L. K., DiCarlo, C. F., & Willingham, T. D. (2022). *Productivity and publishing: Writing processes for new scholars and researchers*. Sage.

Goodman Chien, K. R. (2023). *"The heart of my professional work": A case study of EdD student experiences and their alignment to program outcomes and graduates' professional practice needs* [Doctoral dissertation, Hamline University]. Digital Commons @ Hamline. https://digitalcommons.hamline.edu/hse_all/4577/

hooks, b. (1994). *Teaching to transgress: Education as the practice of freedom*. Routledge.

Kvam, E. K. (2018) Untapped learning potential? A study of teachers' conversations with colleagues in primary schools in Norway. *Cambridge Journal of Education*, 48(6), 697–714. doi: 10.1080/0305764X.2017.1418833

Moroz, K., Harvey, T., & Carlson, J. (2022). *Effective learning environments in higher education online settings: Establishing social presence*. Information Age Publishing.

Piaget, J. (1964). Cognitive development in children: Development and learning. *Journal of Research in Science Teaching*, 2, 176–186.

Putnam, R. D., & Feldstein, L. M. (2004). *Better together: Restoring the American community*. Simon and Schuster.

Vygotsky, L. S. (1978). *Mind in society: The development of higher psychological processes*. Harvard University Press.

CHAPTER SIX

Framing Your Potential-Based Area of Inquiry:

Why is This Important to Other People? What Are Other Points of View?

The text *They Say, I Say* (Graff & Birkenstein, 2021) has been used throughout graduate studies to help students situate their own arguments in the ongoing academic conversation about their research topic. The quote and images shared next encourage students to frame their arguments in the context of what others have said/are saying about your topic:

> If you don't identify the "they say" you're responding to, your own argument probably won't have a point. Readers will wonder what prompted you to say what you're saying and therefore motivated you to write. As the figure . . . suggests, without a "they say", what you are saying may be clear to your audience, but why you are saying it won't be. (Graff & Birkenstein, 2021, p. 4)

As depicted in the cartoon in Figure 6.1, framing your argument and the potential of your study is a critical first step in the research process. In this step of the process, you will explore your own perspective on the topic, explain the existing academic arguments in the field, and provide the distinctive research pathway to the reader.

Figure 6.1 ***Framing an Argument***

Note. Images used with permission, Graff & Birkenstein, 2021, p. 4

Framing Your Audience: Argument and Explanation

An early step in your research process is to identify the people who are impacted by your issue—these can include students, families, teachers, administrators, policymakers, or community members. Identify the stakeholders related to your issue and consider all the possible ways that your research impacts them. The stakeholders can be identified in the literature and through your own experience with the topic. In the introduction of your research, you need to frame your study as it relates to the different stakeholder groups and consider how each group is impacted.

As you frame this introduction, consider how to engage your reader and your audience. Even if your reader is not one of the identified stakeholders, tell them why they should be invested in your study. The purpose of the introduction is to draw the reader into your work and have them see the value of the research. This can be accomplished with compelling statistics, long-term implications, individual stories or experiences, or connections to other research. For example, suppose you are studying math interventions because students are doing poorly on certain state or federal tests. In that case, you can share math test statistics to help the reader understand the urgency or gravity of the issue.

We had one student who was studying the school-to-prison pipeline and its impact on Black girls. She opened with a story of how her own daughter had received a "ticket" for a minor altercation in school and the journey of expunging her record. By sharing this personal connection to the topic and being vulnerable, she was inviting the reader into her research topic.

As a writer, if you can help the reader see the transferable qualities of your study and its implications on their own work or setting, you will build a strong connection. Or if you can pull them into your study with a personal and compelling story, they will see the importance of the work. Do not hesitate to share your own story and your own passion for the topic. As writers, try to go beyond the "what" to the "so what" to help our readers understand that the topics we are writing about are compelling and need to be investigated. The strongest research papers draw the readers in and help them to see the studies as they relate to the academic discourse and the field of education.

As noted in Chapter Three, you will share your researcher positionality in order to situate your own story and passion related to the topic from an objective and transparent approach. And as noted in the cartoon at the beginning of this chapter, you should also situate your arguments in relation to what is being shared in the literature. This will strengthen your arguments. All research has personal and professional ties to the researcher; our goal is to help you create a study that is real, honest, transparent, and impactful. One step in that process is to understand multiple perspectives.

Literature in Support of Identifying Conflicting Points of View

One of the most difficult parts of research is identifying and understanding the different points of view related to a topic. There are points of view that support your ideas and beliefs, and points of view that challenge your ideas or contradict what you believe. Exploring multiple perspectives, opinions, and beliefs makes you a stronger researcher. McMillan and Schumacher (2009) argued that it is "healthy" to identify "contradictory findings" (pp. 74–75). Healthy is synonymous with well done, sound, whole, and robust—this is how we all want our research to be described. You also want to have a credible study. When thinking of this, we note that Booth et al. (2016) posited:

> You will seem more credible if you show not just that you understand the strengths and limitations of your own argument, but that you also understand and have thought about the alternatives to it. To do that, you have to bring those alternative views into your argument by acknowledging and responding to them. (pp. 144–145)

While it is easy and affirming to find studies that support your research, it is difficult to acknowledge and respond to findings and arguments that contradict your own beliefs. We have worked with many students who bristled at the idea of introducing contradictory arguments into their literature and sharing findings from their own study that did not align with their own beliefs. One graduate student was working to identify a possible pathway for a new licensure requirement related to equity work. This student's greatest growth took place when they recognized the importance of the arguments that disputed the need for the license. By recognizing the challenges and the opposing viewpoints related to the need for the license, this student presented a much stronger final rationale. Another student was researching the retention of art teachers. When the student explained the social isolation that these teachers can experience by having a classroom located at a distance from other classrooms, one of her research committee members argued that teaching from a cart and traveling from room to room in a school could combat this isolation. The student was not a proponent of this solution for social isolation but needed to acknowledge this suggestion and explain why it was not a good solution. Both examples depict the journey, the challenges, and the hard work that are required of the researcher. You will inevitably become personally invested in your research, and these challenging/opposing viewpoints will sometimes feel like personal attacks. But these different perspectives help you to be objective and are opportunities to arrive at stronger findings and conclusions. What "they say" in the literature (Graff & Birkenstein, 2021) should be shared and ultimately helps create a more objective study.

Mertler (2006) discussed *objectivity* in the literature review process. Even though you may have some preconceived notions about what you will find in your study, you should include perspectives and research that "support and contradict your views" (p. 42). Opposing viewpoints exist for many reasons—people bring their lived experiences, economic interests, and personal agendas to topics. If a classroom teacher has had 15–20 years of success with a certain text, strategy, or approach, they are going to have a hard time understanding why a change is needed. A politician representing a conservative district is going to have a different opinion or perspective on educational topics and feel the need to represent and support their constituents. A textbook company creating content for all 50 states has a different perspective than someone creating content for a target audience. Opposition is not right or wrong, it just needs to be explored and understood. There is considerable value in understanding all perspectives; your argument is strengthened when you understand how others may perceive an issue and can explain it. When you are talking to someone about your research and they ask, "But have you thought about . . .?," can you say, "Yes, and . . ."? If so, that is a sign that you have done your homework and fully understand the topic you are planning to research. Your work in the literature review is to uncover as many arguments as possible.

According to Machi and McEvoy (2016), the literature critique should uncover "the gaps, contradictions, omissions, and debates about the research subject that were uncovered by the discovery argument" (p. 109). Instead of only advocating for what is known, the topic must be completely uncovered. In exploring multiple perspectives, you will identify the gap, problem, or potential that exists, and unlock your research question. Once you have identified these multiple points of view, you can start to look for the potential with your topic.

Potential-Based vs. "Problem of Practice"

In our programs, we used to encourage our students to identify the *problem of practice* as a way to frame their research studies. When asking students to identify the *problem*, they were identifying broken processes, faulty approaches, and misunderstood needs they hoped to solve. Henriksen and Richardson (2017) spoke of the value that this approach brings to research, saying, "Problems of practice are both complex and actionable, though they are unlikely to have a single right or wrong solution" (p. 61). These *problems* gave our students a place to start, but we found that this approach was causing our students to approach the world with a deficit mindset from the very start of their research. Davis and Museus (2019) argued that "doctoral students are encouraged to use problems to justify the urgency of their research" (para. 2). A problem-based approach does create urgency and can help to draw the reader into the topic. Using a problem-based approach to identifying your topic is a recommended place to start but, as the researcher, you will have to make sure you do not stay focused on the problem.

Problem-based learning is also used in the classroom with students, which "involves a *bottoms-up approach*, which highlights the reason *why* students are going to be learning what they are about to learn. It provides them with an authentic task that needs to be resolved" (Gazith, 2021, p. 46).

When we both worked as middle school educators, we used problem-based learning with our students. We even asked our middle school students to identify *problems* that needed to be fixed in our content areas, communities, and world. As educators, we are trained to identify and solve problems. This then felt like a natural transition in working in graduate research.

But instead, we found our graduate students framed their work in such a way that they were coming to their topics with a deficit mindset. In other words, our graduate students were finding fault in students, students' families, or cultures—they identified limits and lower expectations instead of hope and possibilities. Driehaus (2022), in a study of white middle-class teachers, identified, "A legacy of placing children of color and poverty at the center of the 'problem' of race and class in education has left us in a holding pattern marked by a prevailing deficit discourse and problematizing of students" (p. 5). When our students were focusing on the problems, they sometimes failed to see the potential.

We also found that the *problem of practice* would eventually become "problem students" or "problem employees" that needed to be fixed. Instead of focusing on broken systems, our students were putting the blame and burden on what they perceived to be broken people.

Research can and should give voice to the *researched*. As Davis and Museus (2019) shared,

> Despite the fact that qualitative research can illuminate pressing issues and center populations whose perspectives and experiences might not otherwise enter particular discourses, we would argue that research does not give voice. Instead, research, especially qualitative inquiry, is a tool to share the already-existing stories of participants that were otherwise silenced by oppressive systems. ("Giving Voice" section)

Qualitative research has given voice to those researched, but a problem-based approach has still limited the power in their stories. You can use research to highlight problems but when you shift to identifying where the potential exists, those voices become much stronger in overcoming oppressive systems. What innovation is needed? What positive change can result? What kind of shift can enhance learning, move the system forward, and/or meet the needs of those in the system? Framing the argument with a potential-based approach is a paradigm shift.

Note. Freerange Stock, 2024

Framing the Argument . . . Toward the Potential

Asking students to see the potential also taps into creativity, similar to what Henriksen and Richardson (2017) found: "Many of our teachers noted how, through the process of using design to address classroom and school issues, they began to see themselves as creative individuals who had the tools to enact change in their context" (p. 63). You still can start the process by identifying problems or challenges that you face in your work, but framing your argument toward the potential requires you to address the system, to consider the process and steps forward, and to fully engage your stakeholders in the study. It can also be a way to help engage the reader in the topic. By framing your study as potential-based, you can help the reader see value in the topic.

A potential-based approach requires a problem-solving approach, as Henriksen and Richardson (2017) shared:

> Educational problems of practice are complex and involve a range of moving parts and variables, including school and classroom contexts, human psychology, and knowledge of pedagogy and content. We argue that when confronted by such complex problems, it helps to take a strategic approach to problem solving, treating it as a systematic process of analyzing and redesigning one's everyday work in schools (from classroom management, to student engagement, to community relations, or parent engagement, and

> more). In doing so, we can adapt some of the approaches and skills that designers have often successfully applied to human centered problems. (pp. 63–64)

In conclusion, you must be intentional and thoughtful about how you frame your research topic. You set the tone for the study and you decide whose voices, perspectives, and stories are included, as well as whose are not. As noted in the Potential-Based Research Framework introduced in Chapter One, "critical reflection" traverses both sides of the mountain. This journey requires your most careful deliberation to arrive at the top!

⇨ Chapter Six Reflective Activities

1. Connection with Stakeholders

Make a list of all stakeholders related to your research study. Identify how your research impacts them. This list will be beneficial when you have completed your study and are considering its implications.

2. Experiential Interview

The purpose of this activity is to help you further investigate your potential-based topic with other professionals/stakeholders. Consider what you would like to know about the issue and develop 5–10 interview questions and list the scholarly sources that helped create the questions. Interview a minimum of two people to better understand your topic. You may conduct these interviews as a focus group (all interviewees sit down together as a group to discuss the topic). Please take detailed notes (you may consider recording the interviews). After the interviews, create a document (graphic organizer, narrative paper, etc.) that shares key information and discusses your findings. Within your document:

a. Explain (briefly) your potential-based topic

b. Share the names of interviewees, their positions, and their relationship to the issue

c. Provide a summary of how interviewees responded to your questions; identify similarities and differences between respondents

d. Reflect on how these interviews have informed your deepened understanding of the issue—What have you learned? What do you still want to know? How has this information impacted your perspective on the issue?

e. Include answers to the following questions: Why is this important to other people? What are other points of view on your problem?

3. Visual Concept Map (Step 1) (Please note: Step 2 will be completed as Reflective Activity #3 in Chapter Seven.)

In this first step of creating a visual concept map, please consider the literature themes that support and challenge your study. Consider what literature establishes a foundation for your study. Where in the existing literature will you begin reading?

Figure 6.2 ***Visual Concept Map Activity: Step 1***

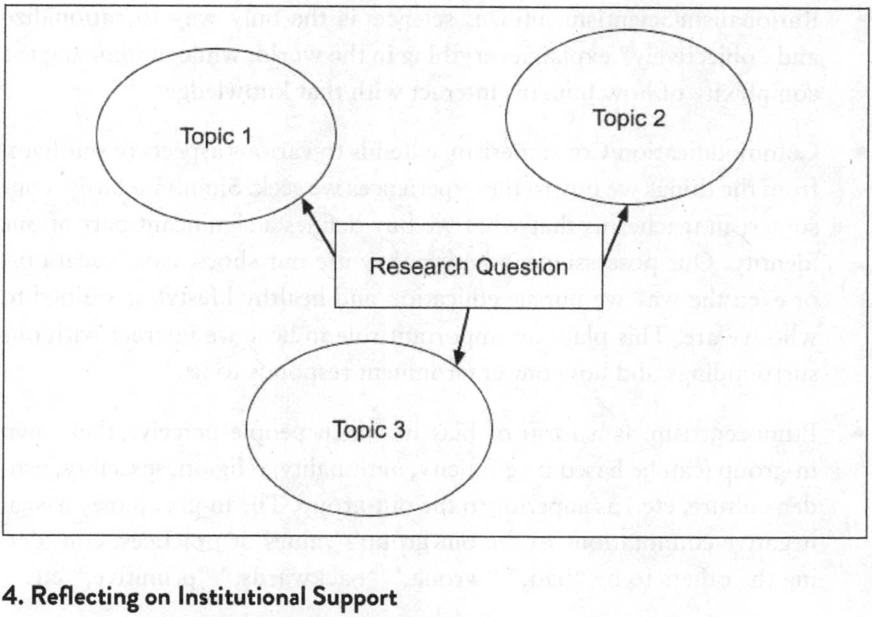

4. Reflecting on Institutional Support

- Identify the goals of your program/organization/institution.
- Reflect on how your research is aligned with these goals.

- In this reflection, also discuss what supports your program/organization/institution has in place to help you with your research.

5. Discourses of Modernity

In their text *Ecojustice Education: Toward Diverse, Democratic, and Sustainable Communities*, Martusewicz et al. (2020, 2024) addressed the concept of modernity by outlining discourses that work together to create a modern "taken-for-granted value-hierarchized worldview" ("Discourses of Modernity" definition). Understanding each of these discourses allows a researcher to more fully frame the scope of their study.

- Individualism: assumes that people can meet their greatest potential by working independently. Following this discourse, people pursue their own self-interests by accumulating wealth or other resources.
- Progress: the belief that change is inevitable, linear, essential, and overall beneficial to societal growth.
- Rationalism/Scientism: utilizes science as the only way to rationalize and "objectively" explain everything in the world, while minimizing the complexity of how humans interact with that knowledge.
- Commodification/Consumerism: extends to various aspects of our lives, from the things we buy to the experiences we seek. Simultaneously, consumerism teaches us that what we buy defines a significant part of our identity. Our possessions, whether they are our shoes, cars, vacations, or even the way we pursue education and healthy lifestyles, are tied to who we are. This plays an important role in how we interact with our surroundings and how our environment responds to us.
- Ethnocentrism: is a form of bias in which people perceive their own in-group (can be based on ethnicity, nationality, religion, sexuality, gender, culture, etc.) as superior to the out-group. The in-group may assign negative connotations to the out-group's values or practices, considering the others to be "bad," "wrong," "backwards," "primitive," etc.

We encourage you to review your potential-based topic through each of these discourses. To do so, list 3–5 examples of how each discourse plays out in society, paying particular attention to educational contexts: schools, or informal education settings. While doing so, please consider any *hidden curriculum* involved that could impact learners. The Great Schools Partnership (2015) explained that hidden curricula are the "unspoken or implicit academic, social, and cultural messages that are communicated to students while they are in school" ("Hidden curriculum"). Next, explore how the examples are interconnected and reflect on possible connections to your potential-based research topic.

Table 6.1 ***Discourses of Modernity***

Discourse and abbreviated description	**Examples of how this plays out in society**	**Connection to your potential-based research topic**
Individualism: People meet their greatest potential by working independently. They pursue their own self-interests by accumulating wealth or other resources.		
Progress: Change is inevitable, linear, essential, and overall beneficial to societal growth.		
Rationalism/Scientism: Science is the only way to rationalize and "objectively" explain everything in the world.		
Commodification/Consumerism: Teaches us that what we buy defines a significant part of our identity. This plays an important role in how we interact with our surroundings and how our environment responds to us.		
Ethnocentrism: A form of bias in which people perceive their own in-group (can be based on ethnicity, nationality, religion, sexuality, gender, culture, etc.) as superior to the out-group.		

6. Identifying Counterarguments

Use ChatGPT or another AI tool to identify counterarguments for your research topic. For example, if you are researching how to implement restorative practices in the classroom, what do opponents of restorative practices argue and/or what are the challenges associated with implementing restorative practices?

7. Where Are You on the Mountain? Assessment of Conditions

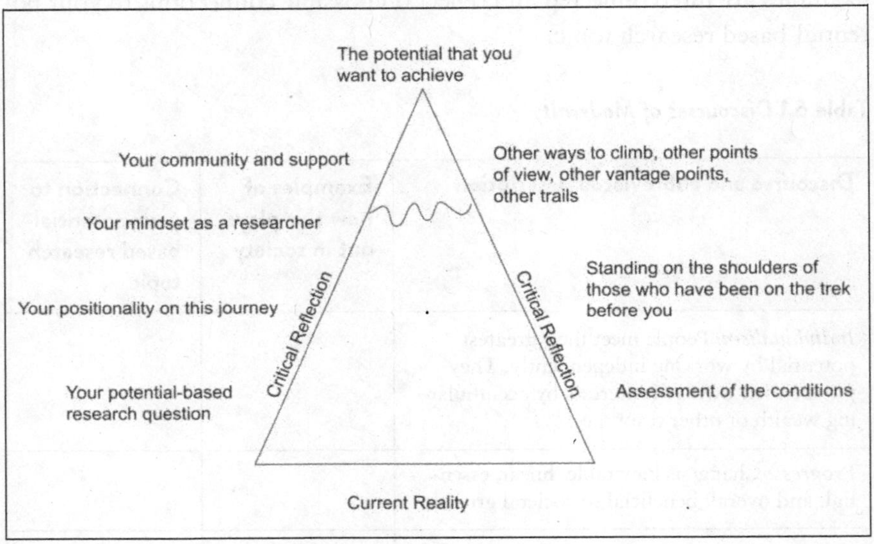

Find time this week to go for a walk (or engage in another activity that allows you to think). As you do this, reflect on what you have discovered about how others perceive a given journey and how that potentially differs from your own approach to the same or similar journey. Thinking about your own potential-based research topic, what varied perspectives influence how the topic is perceived and/or has been approached by others? What does this, then, mean for you and your research?

References

Booth, W. C., Colomb, G. G., Williams, J. M., Bizup, J., & Fitzgerald, W. T. (2016). *The craft of research* (4th ed). University of Chicago Press.

Davis, L. P., & Museus, S. D. (2019, July 19). *Identifying and disrupting deficit thinking.* Medium. https://medium.com/national-center-for-institutional-diversity/identifying-and-disrupting-deficit-thinking-cbc6da326995

Driehaus, T. (2022). *Blinded by whiteness: Middle-class white teachers' explorations of identity and deficit discourse at the intersection of race, class, and perceived ability* [Doctoral dissertation, Kutztown University of Pennsylvania]. Research Commons: Kutztown University. https://research.library.kutztown.edu/edddissertations/24

Freerange Stock. (2024). *Hiking-and-climbing-on-mountain* [Photograph]. iStock Getty Images. https://freerangestock.com/photos/128038/hiking-and-climbing-on-mountain-.html

Gazith, K. (2021). *Teaching with purpose: How to thoughtfully implement evidence-based practices in your classroom*. Solution Tree Press.

Graff, G., & Birkenstein, C. (2021). *They say/I say* (5th ed.). W. W. Norton & Company.

Great Schools Partnership. (2015, July 13). *Hidden curriculum*. The Glossary of Education Reform. https://www.edglossary.org/hidden-curriculum/

Henriksen, D., & Richardson, C. (2017). Teachers are designers: Addressing problems of practice in education. *Phi Delta Kappan, 99*(2), 60–64. https://doi.org/10.1177/0031721717734192

Machi, L. A., & McEvoy, B. T. (2016). *The literature review: Six steps to success* (3rd ed.). Corwin.

Martusewicz, R., Edmundson, J., & Lupinacci, J. (2020). *Ecojustice education: Toward diverse, democratic, and sustainable communities* (3rd ed.). Routledge.

Martusewicz, R., Edmundson, J., & Lupinacci, J. (2024). "Conceptual toolbox." *Ecojustice education: Toward diverse, democratic, and sustainable communities*. Routledge. https://routledgetextbooks.com/textbooks/9781138018846/toolbox.php

McMillan, J., & Schumacher, S. (2009). *Research in education: Evidence based inquiry* (7th ed.). Pearson.

Mertler, C. A. (2006). *Action research: Teachers as researchers in the classroom*. Sage.

CHAPTER SEVEN

Standing on the Shoulders of Those Who Came Before

We borrow this chapter title from the book, **The Power of Questions** *by Falk and Blumenreich (2005), a text dedicated to exploring teacher and student research in the classroom. We believe the metaphor of standing on the shoulders of others is the perfect way to envision the literature review process. Other empirical studies will hold you up . . . other arguments and conclusions will elevate and develop your own thoughts . . . other researchers will set the foundation for your own work. The quote that follows is another way to think about the literature review. A conversation that you are about to enter. . . .*

> *Imagine that you enter a parlor. You come late. When you arrive, others have long preceded you, and they are engaged in a heated discussion, a discussion too heated for them to pause and tell you exactly what it is about. In fact, the discussion had already begun long before any of them got there, so that no one present is qualified to retrace for you all the steps that had gone before. You listen for a while, until you decide that you have caught the tenor of the argument; then you put in your oar. Someone answers; you answer him; another comes to your defense; another aligns himself against you, to either the embarrassment or gratification of your opponent, depending upon the quality of your ally's assistance. However, the discussion is interminable. The hour grows late, you must depart. And you do depart, with the discussion still vigorously in progress.*
>
> *—Kenneth Burke, The Philosophy of Literary Form (1974, pp. 110–111)*

Those That Came Before Us: Argument and Explanation

NOW THAT YOU HAVE a rudimentary start on your research topic, it is time to explore the supporting literature. You should move into this stage of your research with an understanding of the importance of using literature to support your study. Additionally, you should move into this stage as soon as possible—start reading, reading, and reading. There are two main reasons to begin reading the related literature: First, make sure you have the right research topic. . . . Do the literature and research maintain your interest and enthusiasm? Can you stay committed to this topic for the time needed to complete your research? And second, begin gathering the knowledge, vernacular, and arguments. Enter the scholarly conversation.

As you begin to write your arguments and declarative statements related to the literature on your research topic, you should always be asking yourself, "says who?" In working with our students, we find that they talk about feeling accomplished and scholarly when they run across a citation or quote in a source and have already read works from the same researcher or theorist. Feeling accomplished or scholarly in these moments helps to balance the moments when the literature review can feel daunting and overwhelming. The literature process is often the most difficult part of the research process for students, but there are ways to make it a bit more attainable. We are going to share ideas and considerations that we have learned from years of working with our students.

An early step in the literature process should be to identify all the keywords related to your study. Begin by making a list of related words or controlled vocabulary to help in the browsing and search stage of gathering literature. A *controlled vocabulary* is an organized list of terms and phrases you use when browsing databases or searching for literature. You will most likely use a thesaurus to identify related terms. When you find an article in a database that is related to your topic, take note of the listed keywords or descriptors. For example, we do quite a bit of research on social presence in online learning. In Figure 7.1 that we share next, you can see the list of descriptors in the description of a research article we found on *social presence*. In addition to using *social presence* when we search for related research, we have an additional list of keywords we can use.

Figure 7.1 *Descriptors Listed for a Research Article on Social Presence in ERIC Database*

Descriptors: Distance Education, Online Courses, Learning Motivation, Student Attitudes, Electronic Learning, Communities of Practice, Preservice Teachers, Elementary Education, Foreign Countries, Asynchronous Communication, Self Efficacy, Learning Strategies, Teacher Student Relationship, Interpersonal Relationship

Start exploring databases, which are the digital libraries of peer-reviewed articles and empirical studies related to your research topic. Work to become as familiar as possible with your institution's library and tools. Spend some time at the library; lean on the human resources available to you, and remember that most libraries have excellent work areas. Exhaust the tools available to you. Your tuition dollars are hard at work, providing you access to databases and interlibrary loan services; please be sure to utilize those resources. Make an appointment with the academic librarian assigned to your field and let them show you where and how to search your institution's tools and sources. We have an academic librarian assigned to our department; when one of our doctoral students was struggling to find empirical research to support one of her literature themes, she spent an entire afternoon meeting with our academic librarian. She walked out of the library with 15+ empirical studies and a wealth of knowledge and strategies for searching databases. She benefited from her time at the library; we encourage you to make the most of your library resources, as well.

It is also necessary to balance empirical studies and articles that present theoretical arguments. Theoretical arguments are made by experts in the field, while empirical studies are actual research projects that provide observed, measured, and experienced understanding of your topic. You will include both in your literature. The framework for your study will be based on your exhaustive review of the literature; you will either develop a conceptual framework for your research based on the literature that you read or you will use an existing theoretical framework to guide your study. But you will not be able to determine this until you have immersed yourself in the literature. A bonus of reading empirical studies is that the authors typically identify areas for future research in the conclusion of their studies—this can help to justify and validate the urgency of your own study.

Another crucial step in the literature process is to intentionally design a system for organizing your literature sources. The majority of our students use some type of electronic organization system—where articles and studies are stored electronically (files are organized by authors' names). Many students also create some type of document or spreadsheet where they collect quotes and annotated reviews of literature. A few students will print their sources. The key is to figure out what works best *for you*. There are systems and tools that you can purchase. We encourage you to spend time on this important step. Even as we were working on this text, there were times that we used a direct quote or referenced a text but forgot to put the source in our own Google folder (*our system!*). Unfortunately, we have spent hours trying to find a direct quote that we have used or trying to locate a source that was cited. Please follow this important step better than we have!

Before you begin reading, you will identify potential topics in the literature. As you continue reading, it is helpful to build a Visual Concept Map (see Reflective Activity #3 at the end of this chapter) or a literature outline. Create a visual way to depict your literature path in support of your research topic. You might start this activity by brainstorming every possible topic that supports your research, but fine-tuning this map to ONLY the topics that support your study can be challenging. Often, we discuss the "rabbit hole" during the literature process. You start reading literature that detracts from your actual research study. Because you are invested and passionate about your topic, everything you read is interesting and compelling. But it is not all related to your study. When you read an article that is interesting but is taking you down the rabbit hole, you do not have to get rid of it—designate a folder for post-research reading.

Last, we mentioned this when discussing a "system" for literature, you should write summaries and gather quotes as you read literature. Time is precious—there is no need to read an article more than once. Before you start the review of relevant literature, determine where and how you will record the literature that you read. We have revised and implemented these steps with hundreds of our graduate students during the literature review process. White (2017) reminded us, "Notice that *nothing* about paying these dues . . . is about writing; it's about spending the time required to do all the reading and pre-work in preparation for the writing" (p. 264). Spending time immersed in the literature and completing the pre-work is how you build the foundation to address your proposed research topic. We have found that early work with the literature is extremely beneficial: For example, in our doctoral program, we moved the written exam into the first year of graduate work and revised the exam to be a preliminary review of the literature based on individual, rudimentary, student-selected research questions. The results were increased readiness, shorter research completion timelines, and better-focused studies.

Literature in Support of . . . Literature!

Reviewing literature is a foundation for your study. You are crafting and building an argument in support of your study. Mertler (2006) stated that the literature "allows you to use the insights and discoveries of others whose research came before yours in order to make your research more efficient and effective" (p. 40). You can use the literature and research of others to keep your own study narrow and focused.

There are several purposes for your examination of existing literature. The literature establishes the background context on your topic by establishing what research has already been done on the topic. You should include seminal theories and research on the topic. The literature also helps to define key terms and to explain relationships between elements of your study. As you unpack related research and theories related to your topic, you will find support and opposition for your approach. This will help you to focus the wording of your research question(s) and clarify your purpose. The reader of your literature review should understand and be familiar with the existing literature on your topic by the time they finish reading your literature review section.

During the process of immersing yourself in the literature, you gain incredible understanding and knowledge about your topic. Mills (2003) discussed how to situate oneself in the literature that is being read:

> Taking time to immerse yourself in the literature allows you to reflect on your own problems through someone else's lens. You can locate yourself within the research literature and find support for what you are doing or be challenged by what other researchers have done and how they have tackled a particular problem. (p. 29)

You are increasing your expertise in the field from other researchers and gaining understanding from those who have already completed the research journey. Previous research virtually always concludes with recommendations for future research. You may find justification for your study from previous research.

There is a community of scholars who share your passion and interest. The literature, as Palmer (1998) argued, is a way to join a community that supports your research. Palmer stated,

> We need to know the current conclusions in order to get in on the conversation. But it is not our knowledge of conclusions that keeps us in the truth. It is our commitment to the conversation itself, our willingness to put forward our observations and interpretations for testing by the community and to return the favor to others. To be in the truth, we must know how to observe and reflect and speak and listen, with passion and with discipline, in the circle gathered around a given subject. (p. 104)

As you join the literature circle on your research topic, consider your commitments and your willingness to share with the broader research community. You will know that you have selected the right research topic by gauging your passion for joining this circle.

Note. Photograph taken by author, Harvey (2024).

Mertler (2006) stated that the literature is integrated into every aspect of your research—and at this point in your research process, most importantly, the literature should help you with the broad development of your research question, the narrowing of that question, and the background information that establishes a foundation for your study. The following reflective activities are designed to help you reach these outcomes.

⇨ Chapter Seven Reflective Activities

1. Infographic Activity

Create an infographic that includes the following information:

- What is/are your research question(s)?
- Who are you? (Explain your positionality to the topic.)
- Why do you care about the topic? (Explain your connection to the topic.)
- Who is your community of support?
- What is your research paradigm?
- Who is your audience?
- Who does your research benefit? Where is the potential?
- What literature supports your topic?
- What are other points of view on your topic?
- How can you answer your question(s)? (Explain your initial ideas around data collection.)

2. 60-Second Radio Spot

This activity allows you to find key information and share it in a concise and creative manner. Develop who, what, when, where, why, and how questions and answers related to your potential-based research focus. Then create a 60-second radio spot and present it to the class. It is important not to turn this into a television script; instead, really focus on the content, and remember that a radio audience will hear only your summary (answers to the 5W-How questions). Be creative in how you use your radio time (i.e., song, interview, commercial, sportscast).

3. Visual Concept Map (Step 2) (Please note: Step 1 was completed as Reflective Activity #3 in Chapter Six.)

In the second step of creating a visual concept map, please expand your concept map to include subtopics.

Figure 7.2 *Visual Concept Map Activity: Step 2*

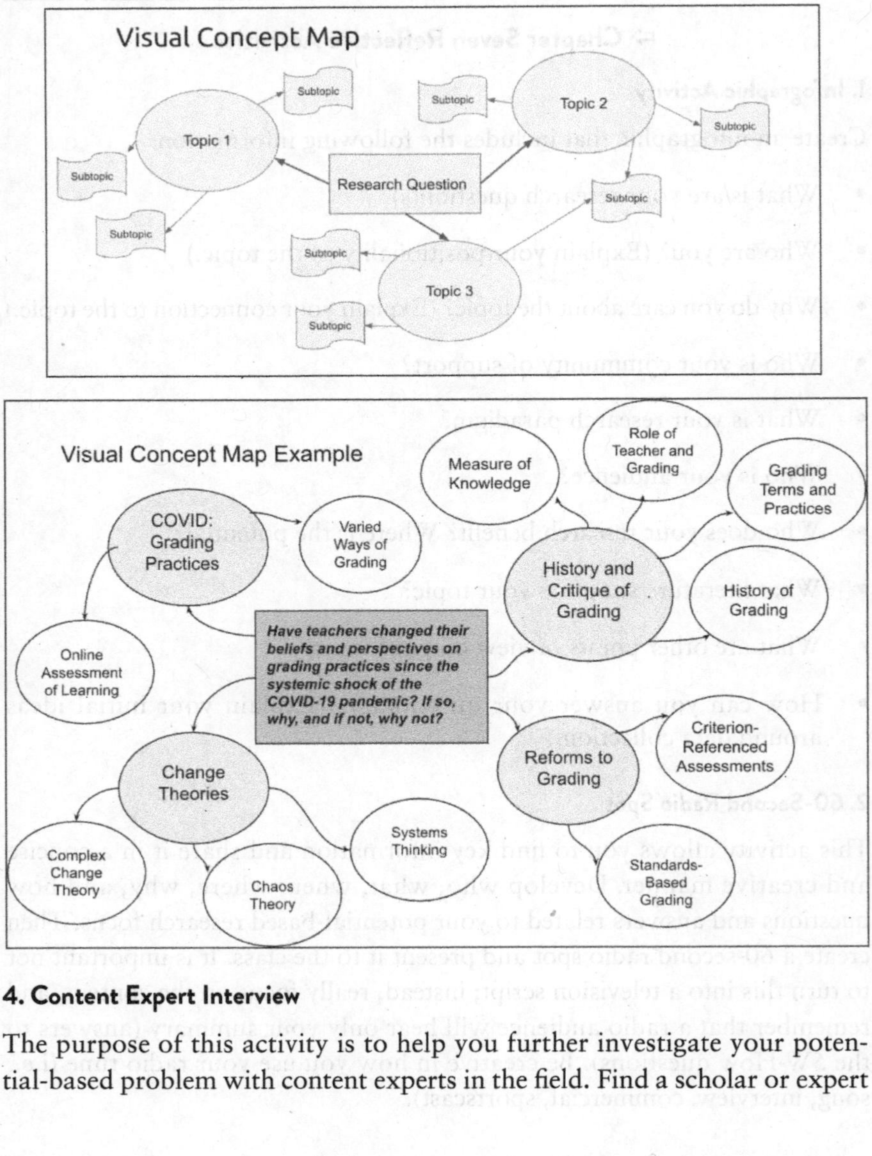

4. Content Expert Interview

The purpose of this activity is to help you further investigate your potential-based problem with content experts in the field. Find a scholar or expert in the field and draft 5–10 interview questions about your topic. Interview this person, keeping in mind that through this interview both you and the person being interviewed may be pushed to think of your original ideas in a new way—through the lens of potential-based research. Please take detailed notes (you may consider recording the interviews). After the interviews, write a short reflection where you:

a. State your research topic.
b. Explain the content expertise of your interviewee. Share the name(s) of interviewee(s), their position(s), the date(s) of the interview(s), and their relationship to the issue.
c. Summarize how the interviewee responded to your questions; identify in what ways you both were pushed to think differently about the topic, and explain new insights following this conversation.
d. Reflect on how this interview has informed your deepened understanding of the issue—What have you learned? What do you still want to know? How has this information impacted your perspective on the issue?

5. Where Are You on the Mountain? Assessment of Conditions

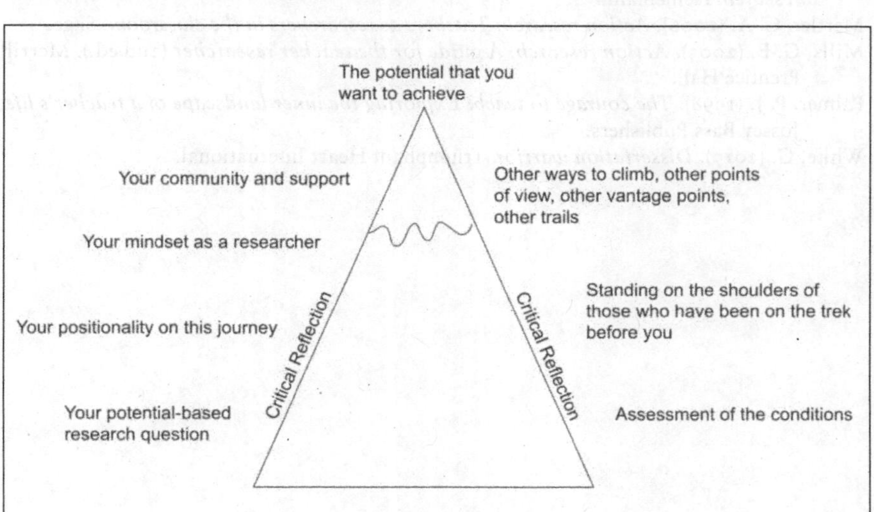

You have spent more time now with your potential-based topic and have reviewed what others have discovered about it. Reflect on the following questions:

- Has this information shifted your own thinking?
- What is your current mindset toward your topic?
- How did reading the work of others committed to this topic impact you as a researcher? Were there specific texts that invited you to think of the topic from a different point of view, wonder about other ways to approach the work ahead of you, or decide that perhaps you need to be traveling on a different trail (exploring a different topic altogether or a different aspect of your current topic)?

Please take time to reflect on each of these questions individually and then create a literature "to do" list—then capture your ideas for next steps regarding your exploration of the potential-based topic you are interested in.

References

Burke, K. (1974). *The philosophy of literary form.* University of California Press.

Falk, B., & Blumenreich, M. (2005). *The power of questions: A guide to student and teacher research.* Heinemann.

Mertler, C. A. (2006). *Action research: Teachers as researchers in the classroom.* Sage.

Mills, G. E. (2003). *Action research: A guide for the teacher researcher* (2nd ed.). Merrill Prentice Hall.

Palmer, P. J. (1998). *The courage to teach: Exploring the inner landscape of a teacher's life.* Jossey Bass Publishers.

White, G. (2017). *Dissertation warrior.* Triumphant Heart International.

CHAPTER EIGHT

Nuts and Bolts & Conclusion

Our meeting began with excitement. The student was engaged in her topic and ready to share her proposal with her dissertation committee. Committee members were engaged and ready to support the work. As the meeting progressed a committee member asked about why the student chose to use a particular sub-heading; the committee member was not only seeking further clarification about the student's topic, but also (unconsciously or consciously) seeking clarity on how the process our university employs may be different than the process she herself had gone through as she wrote her dissertation at a different institution. As the chair of the committee, I (Karen) welcomed the committee member's question and was eager to have the student share her rationale for the sub-heading as a springboard, then, for further conversation about the overall project and process. Unfortunately, either because the student was nervous or because she had not fully thought through the "why" behind each part of her projected dissertation and how each section supported the topic, her response halted conversation and in many ways reflected poorly on the program. Instead of talking through her thought process and rationalizing how the sub-topic was positioned in the context of the larger potential-based topic, she responded with, "I just looked at lots of [my University's] dissertations and followed how other people did their sections." It was a missed opportunity for this student. Rather than "owning" the structure and the topic, she conveyed a "jumping through the hoops" formulaic approach to the research. It was a disheartening moment as a chair.

Nuts and Bolts: Argument and Explanation

As was shared early in this book, our goal in writing this was to launch your research and writing. It was not to discuss the methods for your research or to walk you through the entire dissertation process. At this time, however, we do believe it is helpful to look at where you are, and through this chapter's reflective activities, to look ahead to where you are going to avoid the formulaic approach described in the opening vignette. Understanding where you are going increases *your* "owning" of the structure and topic. What is asked of you in the next chapters of your dissertation? What will your literature review and actual research study entail? Knowing where you are going will help you take the next steps and will help "confirm" that you have chosen a topic that will continue to hold your interest and propel you through the process with true potential always front-of-mind. If you are still wavering on topic selection, we encourage you at this point to allow a set amount of time to live in the various topics you are considering but to then, once that short allocated time is up, move on—choose a topic and write! Remember that while choosing a potential-based topic that is relevant and meaningful to you is important, there is not ONE "right" topic—choose one and move! Take time now to fully operationalize the process that lies before you; determine how your end product will be assessed, seek clarity about the structure of your dissertation, and set goals that will ensure you successfully complete this important work.

The "eye on the prize" mantra definitely comes into play as you take the next steps in moving your potential-based topic through the ongoing review of literature, the data collection, and the sharing of results. Knowing up front how your end product will be assessed allows you to "pack" properly and to be fueled by a desire to achieve the excellence outlined in the assessment tool.

As you complete this review, you will more than likely find that the rubric or other assessment tool used is divided in a manner that aligns to the structure your institution recommends or requires of the resulting publication. Taking time now to understand this structure, to more fully understand the "why" of each section, to seek clarification, and to create documents that serve as a template for the ensuing work, allows you to avoid unnecessary backtracking or retracing of steps later in the process. Indeed you are creating the map that will take you from the base to the summit.

While understanding the ending is necessary and helpful, it may also add a new layer of doubt and/or a sense of being overwhelmed. We encourage you to lean into these fears. They are real, and the climb will be challenging, but you are up to the challenge. Taking time now to set specific goals through the creation of a timeline will help you chunk the work, with each "smaller" task feeling manageable. Sharing this timeline with members of your community of support will give everyone a sense of what is next and will provide a measure of accountability.

This is your journey: Enjoy it! Remember that through identifying a strong potential-based topic you have already taken a huge step in completing your dissertation, a step that should propel your desire and ability to take your important topic and share it with others. You will hit "landslides" as you journey up the mountain, but your backpack is full of what you need, you are adequately nourished, and you are ready to journey on to the summit. Taking heart in the title of Block's (2003) book, *The Answer to How is Yes: Acting on What Matters*, you will get moving and realize you have the tools to complete this journey.

⇨ Chapter Eight Reflective Activities

1. Assessment

Locate and review the rubric/checklist that your institution uses to assess your final product. Write down any questions you have about the assessment tool. These questions will be the basis of a large-group discussion in class.

2. Study the Existing Products

Locate 5–10 dissertations or finished research studies from your institution and review the structure of each, using the questions that follow to guide your review:

- What is the purpose of each chapter?
- How are chapters organized? Why do you think that is?
- How are headings used to organize information and guide readers?
- What are some possible headings that should be included in your own dissertation?

3. Outline Your Final Product

Create an outline of your chapters. This outline should follow the structure you have identified. The actual content can be very "loose"—after all, you are in the early stages of this process. It is important however that you start asking yourself why each idea you are including should indeed be included. Doing so early in this process will ensure that your dissertation is organized, thorough, and relevant, and that you are able to provide a rationale for each part of your writing instead of saying, "I included it because that's what other people did."

4. Table of Contents

Using your outline developed in Reflective Exercise #3, build a Google Table of Contents (https://www.youtube.com/watch?v=SI62ulNYkL8). Embedding this formatting tool into your document now ensures easy navigation for you as the writer and for the committee of readers that will be reviewing the on-going work.

5. Timeline

Think realistically about what needs to happen in order for you to complete this project and create a timeline. We invite you to complete and share the Dissertation Planning Timeline (https://docs.google.com/document/d/1fao9OOI72Il_K2WWaohcuaz-dmD4Fj8YAqU5Tym4fZI/edit).

6. What Do You Need?

With your timeline in mind (Reflective Activity #5), reflect on your needs as a writer. Dowell et al. (2022) encouraged writers to "examine when you have time to write and what might be consuming your time" (p. 24). By doing so, "you can set a realistic writing schedule and establish a writing routine that works for you" (Dowell et al., 2022, p. 24). Within this activity, spend three days taking note of how you use your time. We advise that you choose a three-day span that includes weekday and weekend days and that you find a way to document your activities hour-by-hour.

Next, review the findings and analyze common trends. Use these trends, then, to determine what time of day you have the "right amount" of distraction and adequate privacy to write and/or what parts of your "typical" day can be adjusted to create space for the important writing work ahead of you. Analyze, too, the environments you tend to exist in and work to determine which are most conducive to the type of focus necessary for strong academic writing. It may be that this is your time to change a space in your house, to create a space you want to use as your writing haven, or to find a spot in your community that is open at your ideal writing time and not only conducive but inviting.

The more you can identify and/or create settings that you want to be in, the more likely you are to go there at the designated time and motivate yourself through your ongoing progress. It is important to know yourself and to remember that "writing is highly personal, and every writer needs to figure out what they need, where they write best, and when they are the most productive" (Dowell et al., 2022, p. 15). Choose someone from your community of support and talk with them about what you discovered through this activity. Focus your conversation on what steps you intend to take to make time to do scholarly writing.

7. Let's Do It!

- Revisit the content of the dissertations you secured in Reflective Activity #2 with specific focus on each dissertation's Chapter One.
- Revisit your drafted outline.
- You are ready. . . . Draft YOUR Chapter One!

8. Assess Your Writing Process

Read the following questions that focus exclusively on the process of writing. Then reread your drafted Chapter One with these questions in mind. Reflect on each question, write short responses to at least two of them, and be ready to share your responses in a small group of fellow writers. After having that discussion, think about what within your classmates' processes you would like to try in your next writing session?

- What process did you go through to produce this piece of writing?
- What problems did you encounter while you were working on it? How did you solve them?

- What was especially satisfying to you about the process?
- What did you find frustrating about the process?
- What were your goals for creating this piece of work? Did your goals change as you worked on it? Did you meet your goals?
- What did writing your draft of Chapter One reveal about you as a writer and learner? (ex. how you learn best, what you enjoy, what is easy, what is hard, etc.)

—Adapted from Taylor, 2022

9. Assess Your Scholarly Writing

After discussing your own writing process with a small group (Reflective Activity #8), take time to assess your actual writing:

- How do you feel about this piece of writing?
- What parts of it do you particularly like? Dislike? Why?
- What is the one thing you want people to notice when they look at your work?

—Adapted from Taylor, 2022

10a. You As a Scholarly Writer

Who are you as a scholarly writer and what resources are there to support your ongoing growth? Take time to reflect individually on the following questions:

- How do you perceive yourself as a scholarly writer?
- What do you like about research and scholarly writing?
- What do you dislike about research and scholarly writing?
- What are your writing strengths as they relate to academic expository writing?
- What are your writing weaknesses as they relate to academic expository writing?

- How do you know when your scholarly writing is good?
- What aspects of academic writing do you find the most challenging? To answer this question, reflect upon the list of writing tasks listed next and identify **at least three areas** for your future growth and development. Discuss why you selected each, and prioritize them in order of importance to you.
  - Discovering or refining a topic
  - Constructing a thesis
  - Researching a topic
  - Finding evidence
  - Evaluating evidence
  - Synthesizing and integrating research
  - Supporting ideas with primary sources
  - Making broad generalizations that are clear and connected to primary sources
  - Developing ideas
  - Supporting ideas
  - Organizing ideas
  - Clarifying ideas
  - Striving for conciseness, (i.e., avoiding the use of inflated or empty phrases)
  - Considering your audience
  - Removing clutter
  - Crafting a lead and/or an ending
  - Embedding examples from your professional experience

- Connecting theory to practice and making this connection explicit
- Improving transitions (between sentences and/or paragraphs)
- Focusing on sentence structure (run-ons, fragments, etc.)
- Focusing on paragraph structure (unity, topic sentences, etc.)
- Integrating direct and indirect quotes, (i.e., explicit attribution)
- Formatting (font, type size, margins, etc.)
- Including citations

10b. You As a Scholarly Writer

In class, join with others who have identified similar areas of growth. Collectively discuss this skill set and locate two or three resources that can support you (and others) as they work to achieve that aspect of scholarly writing. Be prepared to share those resources with others.

11. Where Are You on the Mountain? Assessment of Conditions

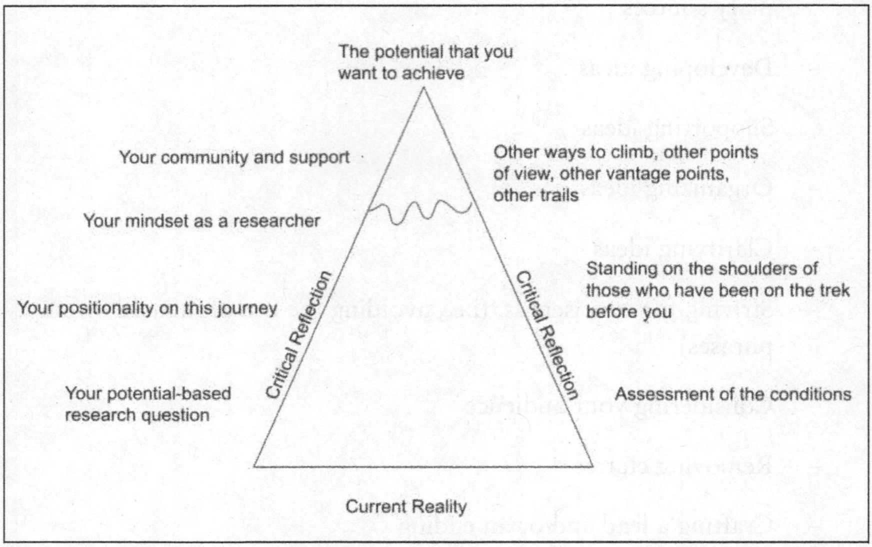

You, *yes you*, are at the top of the Potential-Based Research Framework mountain. You have your topic and you are focused on the potential that lies within your research of that topic. Now you need to prepare fully for the journey that lies ahead, one that we believe can be best visualized through the creation of your next itinerary and packing list. Will you be climbing another mountain? Journeying down a fast moving river? Exploring a dense forest? Whatever metaphor you decide fits you as a researcher and your research—use it to your benefit. It may even help to create a framework of your own that utilizes the metaphor you choose, illustrating key aspects of the journey that will allow you to be successful in reaching the next destination.

References

Block, P. (2003). *The answer to how is yes: Acting on what matters.* Berrett-Koehler Publishers, Inc.

Dowell, M.-M., Saal, L. K., DiCarlo, C. F., & Willingham, T. D. (2022). *Productivity and publishing: Writing processes for new scholars and researchers.* Sage.

Taylor, M. (2022). *How to encourage students to reflect on their writing.* Imagination Soup. https://imaginationsoup.net/encourage-students-to-reflect-on-their-writing/

ABOUT THE AUTHORS

TRISH HARVEY is an associate professor in the School of Education with an emphasis in Advanced Learning Technologies at Hamline University. Trish's background includes over 21 years of K–16 experience including teaching social studies, facilitating graduate students in their pursuit of advanced degrees, and serving as a district digital learning administrator. Her technology-related experiences include a 1-1 iPad implementation roll-out, the development of online and hybrid courses, district-wide professional development around technology goals, and a Bring-Your-Own-Device district initiative. Focus areas of scholarship and research include: the use of digital tools for learning and assessment, fostering quality online learning experiences and relationships between students and instructors, and educational transformation via policy and technology. In her higher education experience, she has advised over 300 capstone students and dissertation students to completion. Additionally, Dr. Harvey serves as the program director for the EdD and MAEd programs where she teaches all research courses.

KAREN MOROZ taught seventh grade for 15 years and then served as a secondary-level literacy coach. She is now an associate professor in and the program director for Hamline's Masters in the Arts of Literacy Education and Reading License programs; she also teaches within the doctoral program. Dr. Moroz's key areas of scholarship include: effective online teaching, engaged learning, formative assessment, technology-enhanced instruction, and facilitating relevant and authentic dialogue with learners. In her role as an instructor within a graduate school, Karen has advised over 200 capstone and dissertation students, providing her with a wealth of understanding of the processes and nuances researchers experience throughout their journey.

INDEX